Desperately Seeking Exclusivity

CHRISTOPHER MARKLAND

Second Printing, 2016

ISBN-13: 978-1-5086-5653-1

ISBN-10: 1-5086-5653-3

Cover Design: Determined Books
Photography by: Larry M. Newton
Cover Model: April Smith

www.DeterminedBooks.com
Facebook.com/determinedbooks
Email: Info@DeterminedBooks.com

www.ChristopherMarkland.com
Facebook: Author Christopher Markland
Instagram: @AuthorChristopherMarkland
Email: Christopher@DeterminedBooks.com

To Brandon, Britt, Jay, and Poot. Love ya'll!

Stephanie, even though this book has
nothing to do with you, everything that I do is about you.

Acknowledgements

To my mother, Jackie, who has always encouraged me, stood behind me, and been there for me, no matter what. I cannot thank you enough. Love you, Lady.

To my family, Lianne, Nikki, Kikki, Heidi, and Erick, thanks for being there for me. Even though we have our issues, our differences, we are still family. I love you all.

To my editor, my friend, Michelle Chester, whose passion for writing and literature inspired me to get up off my butt and finish this novel. Thanks also to Donna Deloney for providing me with insightful feedback to help make this book as good as it could possibly be.

To Anasa Johnson, thank you for your help in being the final set of eyes on this project before it was released. The honor was truly mine.

To my father, Errol Sr., one of the most intelligent men I have ever known. I love you, Sir.

To my homeboys Jack, Gerald, Charles, and Dan, thanks for always being real, for always being true.

To April Smith, thank you for allowing your loveliness to grace the cover of this book. You are a beautiful woman, inside and out.

To Larry "Mike" Newton, thank you for your time, energy, passion and vision in making sure that each shot taken was absolutely the best possible.

To Carl M. Dudley, CMD, thank you for always encouraging me to Chase My Dream. Who Got The Nerve?

Thank you to my beta-readers, Erica, Arnette, Tonya, Octavia, Aaron and especially you, Kiara.

To super-assistant Michelle Gonzalez, thank you for your positive energy.

Thank you to Crystal Evans for helping me to reach everyone possible. I did listen to your advice.

To Boston Davis, "Imagine that". Two of the most powerful words that have ever been spoken.

Thank you Shannon Brown for your help and encouragement.

James Mobley, thank you to you and the team at Multi-Print for always being available, helpful and encouraging. You are truly the definition of networking.

1

Stacey

I said a prayer of thanks as I watched the garage door roll down in front of me. I was so happy that my evening out was over and the date from hell had officially ended.

As I stepped out of the garage and into the foyer of my cozy, three bedroom house, my daughter, Brianna, came rushing out of the kitchen to greet me.

Our little dog, Marco, an excitable package of frenzy disguised as a white toy poodle, was right on her heels, yelping away in excitement.

Cell phone still perched next to her ear, she breathlessly asked above Marco's racket, "So how was it, Mom? How was your date?"

Standing four inches taller than me, putting her at five feet six inches tall, my daughter is a 16-year-old high school junior that is a bundle of energy and enthusiasm who never failed to put a smile on my face. She has a light pecan brown complexion, an athletic build from years of dance classes, and a frizzy afro which was currently wrapped in a head scarf in preparation for her going to bed for the night. I was reluctant to talk about my evening: however, I appreciated her eagerness right about now because I definitely needed it in order to recover from my date from Hell.

"It was an experience," was all I could say in response to her query.

I looked down at what used to be my favorite black cashmere sweater and took in the small white flakes that covered the front of the garment.

Following my eyes, Brianna asked, "What's all that on your sweater?"

"You don't even want to know," I said, leaning wearily against the living room wall.

"I do, Mom. Come on. Tell me, please," she said.

"Have you done your homework? Cleaned up the kitchen?" I asked, desperately trying to distract her. Right about now, the only thing I wanted to do was to get out of my clothes and into bed.

"Yes, ma'am," she responded, a small smile playing on the corners of her mouth. I knew that it was over once I saw that look on her face. I tried another tactic, hoping that would delay the inevitable.

"Aren't you on the phone?" I asked weakly, running out of cards to play in my effort to throw her off the scent.

"Oh!" she said with a yelp of surprise as she looked at the phone in her hand as if it had just suddenly appeared there. "I forgot I was even on it."

She turned her back to me and whispered into the phone. After ending her call, she turned back to face me with a nauseatingly goofy grin on her face.

I shook my head at her and headed towards the couch, Marco bouncing around my ankles with each step.

"So, Mom, tell me all about it," she said, following me into the living room and plopping down on the loveseat across from me. Marco followed her lead and hopped up on to the cushion next to her and propped his head in her lap.

"Okay, okay." I sighed as I kicked off my shoes. "Hold on." I stood up, pulled my cell phone out of my purse, and walked into the kitchen.

For me to be able to relive the experience, I was going to need something to relax me. Just thinking about the past few hours of my evening made me shudder.

I reached up into the cabinet, got out a wine glass, and filled it to the brim from the contents of the bottle of Apothic Red I had opened the night before. I took a long sip before calling my best girlfriend, Angel Troyer.

I smiled wryly to myself when I thought about Angel's name.

Her mother must have known what she had on her hands when she gave birth to Angel to saddle her with that name. My best friend looked like an angel, but she truly had some devilish ways. Tonight for instance, when she set me up on my disaster date the way that she had, was the latest example.

"Hello," Angel said as she answered the phone.

"Heffa!" I responded. "I was getting ready to tell Brianna about my night, so I figured I might as well tell you at the same time."

I pushed the button which activated the speakerphone feature, and the sound of Angel's high-pitched laughter filled the space.

Shaking my head as I walked into the living room, I sat down on the couch next to Brianna. I took another sip of wine and began telling them about my date from Hell.

"Well, I knew it was going to be one of those nights the minute I laid eyes on him. He had an afro that would've made Jimi Hendrix proud," I exclaimed, leaning back against the couch's headrest.

Brianna's laughter mixed with Angel's as they both cracked up. I closed my eyes and took another sip of wine.

I'm going to need a few more refills, I thought, eyeing the bottle sitting on the kitchen counter.

"Anyway," I continued. "This dude was old enough to be Brianna's grandfather. Hell, he was old enough to be my grandfather."

"He had on a bright purple polyester suit with a loud floral print shirt unbuttoned damn near down to his belly button. He was proudly showing off all his taco meat chest hair and fake gold chains. And you know he had the matching purple fedora tilted to the side."

At this point, tears were streaming down Brianna's face as she fell over laughing on the love seat. Angel was hyperventilating with laughter over the speakerphone.

Fortified with another sip of wine, I continued. "Just how Pimp-Daddy-Superfly kept the hat on the 'fro was a miracle in and of itself. At this point, all I could think about was where I was going to bury your body after I finished strangling you the next time I saw you, Angel. How could you set me up on a blind date with this joker? I thought me and you were friends and then you turn around and do this mess to me. Ooh, I was too heated at you."

Angel was laughing so hard that she couldn't even respond.

I glared at the phone for a few seconds and then continued, "Anyway, I kept my game face on and tried to hang in there. I figured I might as well get dinner out of the deal. Well as it turned out, I got two dinners instead of one. This fool would not stop talking with his mouth full and kept spitting food out his damned mouth all night. There was more of his food on my plate than what I had ordered for myself. Look at this mess," I said, pointing to the spots on my ruined sweater.

"Each of these stains is a battle scar from where I was hit with food shrapnel. He was tossing food grenades like we were on a battlefield in Iraq somewhere. I felt like putting on a helmet and yelling, 'INCOMING!' because there were so many food bombs raining down on me."

Brianna was rolling with laughter. The tears were streaming down her cheeks as she lay back on the couch cracking up.

I looked at her and shook my head, listening to them laughing at my night of horror.

"I'm so glad you two are able to find humor in my discomfort," I said in mock anger. Their laughter was becoming contagious and I feigned anger as I tried to continue to fuss at them.

"Here I am taking one for the team with 'Seventies Sam' and y'all are just laughing at me. No kind of sympathy or anything."

"No, Mom," Brianna said in between short breaths. "It's not like that at all. I could just see the look on your face as you tried to eat." She wiped the tears from her eyes.

"Eat?" I yelled out. "There's no way I could've eaten anything while acting like Money Mayweather out there. I was bobbing and weaving all damn night trying to avoid getting hit in the face with flying food."

Angel screamed with laughter at my comment.

"Stop, Mom," Brianna shrieked, her face turning purple with laughter.

"Anyway, little girl," I said, smiling at her as I drained my glass. "This is just too painful for me to continue. Isn't it past your bedtime?"

"Yes, ma'am", she said with a huge grin on her face. "But I want you to tell me how the rest of the date went tomorrow, okay?"

She gathered her school books off the coffee table and headed up the stairs towards her bedroom.

Picking up my phone, I canceled the speakerphone and put it to my ear to continue talking to Angel. She was still laughing, so I gave her a few more moments to compose herself. I glanced at the clock on the stove and saw that it was almost ten. This was the first good thing for me this evening. There was still enough time for me to get plenty of rest so that I could meet with my client in the morning.

After my traumatic evening, I guess my concept of time—hell, reality for that matter—was thrown off.

"You finished laughing over there?" I asked sarcastically, interrupting her.

"Yes, girl. I'm good."

"Glad to hear that. So why didn't you tell me about this guy? You could have given me some kind of warning."

"Girl, I know. I'm sorry about that," she said.

"How could you set me up for the okie-doke like that? You said he was mature. You said that he was tall. You said he was a great conversationalist. What you didn't say was that he was a senior citizen. What you didn't say was that he was barely four feet tall with a twelve inch afro. What you didn't say was that his conversation revolved around his arthritis, his grandkids, and his suits."

"Girl," she said, sounding like she was trying not to start laughing again. "I'm sorry that I did that to you, but I had to."

"You had to?" I exclaimed. "Are you serious? What do you mean you had to?"

"Stacey, he's my boss' older brother who had just come in to town," she offered as an explanation. "My boss wanted me to set him up with one of my single friends who could show him around. You were the first person that came to mind. I needed someone who had a good personality and who could handle herself in any situation. Honestly, I really didn't know too much about him. I just know that if I'd told you what I knew about him, you wouldn't have accepted the invitation."

"You're damn right on that one," I spat.

"See, that's what I'm talking about right there," she said.

"Whatever. I'm getting ready to go to bed," I said. "I'm going to take a shower and wash this food off me. Then I'm going to try to go to sleep and hopefully not have any nightmares about tonight. I've got a showing tomorrow and Lord knows I need some rest after tonight. Just know that you owe me one, girl."

"I know," she said. "I'll make it up to you. I promise. Thank you for doing this for me."

"Mmm hmm," I said and hung up the phone.

After taking a long, hot shower, I lay in my bed surrounded by my thousands and thousands of pillows, looking at the ceiling. I reflected on the new low that my life had sunk to. This was the first real date that I've had in longer than I cared to remember, and it turned out to be a huge disaster.

I knew that Angel meant well and she could have in no way envisioned the type of evening that I ended up having. The fact that I was the first person on her list of single women bothered me.

I was tired of the game, tired of the knuckleheads that seemed to cross my path in the crazy dating scene of metro Atlanta. I knew there were some good brothers out there but I just could not seem to find them. Instead, I get paired up with their pimperish grandfathers.

I shook my head at the idea and drifted off to sleep.

2

Ethan

"Oh, really? Is that so?" I said into the phone as I got up from the couch. I moved the phone from my ear, put it on the arm of the couch, and went to the bathroom.

I relieved myself, washed my hands, dried them carefully, and then returned to the living room. I took my time in doing all of this because I knew from many past experiences that I had all the time in the world.

Sitting back down, I picked up the phone, and sure enough, Antonia Knight, a woman I used to kick it with a few months ago, was still yammering on, not even realizing that I was not on the phone.

I shook my head in disbelief at the fact that she could be so caught up in her own conversation. It seemed she could talk for hours without my input even being necessary.

"Hey, Antonia," I said, interrupting her long-winded story about something involving nothing. "I think someone's about to knock on my door. I'll call you back later."

Not giving her a chance to respond, I quickly pushed the END button on my phone before tossing it on the couch beside me.

Picking up my wireless headset and placing them over my ears, I pushed the START button on the controller to resume the game that I had been playing before being interrupted by Antonia's phone call.

"Ayo, GT," I said into the headset's microphone. "You there?"

A few seconds later, the gruff voice of my friend, Greg Thomas, came through the earpiece.

"Yeah, man. I'm here. I figured you'd gotten scared and quit the game because of this ass whipping that I was handing you," Greg said.

"Quit? Are you serious?" I asked in disbelief. "That word isn't in my vocabulary. Plus, you're barely up by three and it's only halftime."

"Well, let's go then," he said.

Greg and I were playing the latest version of the Madden franchise over the high-speed internet connection that linked our PlayStation game consoles. This had become our usual Friday evening routine for the past few weeks as we both had been in a dating slump lately. He and I would get on the game system and play for hours, unwinding from the long work week, all the while talking to each other about any and every topic ranging from women to work to money.

"I don't even know why I bothered to answer the phone," I said as I pulled up my playbook and selected a pass play so that we could continue our game. "Antonia just doesn't know when to quit. It's been over between us for a long time, but she still wants to act like everything's all good between us."

"I told you about that chick," Greg said. "From the first time I met her, I told you something wasn't right with that woman. But you didn't want to listen."

"I guess," I said grudgingly. Greg had called it correctly in Antonia's case and plenty of others as well. As usual, I didn't heed his advice.

"But anyway," I said, changing the subject. "You know that Walter's looking to buy a house, right?"

"Aww damn!" Greg screamed into his headset as I made a picture-perfect pass to my wide receiver who was uncovered down the field. "I pulled my freakin' safety down to cover your tight-end and left him wide open."

He took a second to calm down before asking, "He's looking for a house, huh?"

"Yessir," I said as I kicked the extra point. "He said that he reached his savings goal and was ready to make the move," I continued as I kicked the ball off to Greg. "I told him that I was going to give my realtor friend, Stacey, a call so that she can try to set something up for him."

"Stacey? How's she doing?" Greg asked with a bit too much indifference.

"She's doing okay, I guess," I said, trying to keep the smile that was spreading across my face from being evident in my voice. "We talked for a while when I called her about Walter and gave her his info. Not too sure about her personal life based on a few of the comments that she made though."

"Oh?" he said with a disinterested tone.

"Don't try to play that hard guy role, negro," I said, laughing. "You know you could've gotten with her when you had the chance. Think about it. She's single, has her own home, her own car, good credit, a business owner, great personality, banging body, the whole nine. But you were kicking it with dingbat Brenda at the time and was all wrapped up in her and all the damn drama she was bringing to you. You brushed Stacey off without giving her a real shot even though for who knows what reason, she was actually interested in your goofy ass."

"First of all, Sir," Greg said, calling me by my nickname as he handed the ball off to his running back and gashed my defense for a nice 37-yard run. "I'm used to women throwing themselves at me. I mean, how can any woman with a pulse not be attracted to these massive arms and broad shoulders? And as for Brenda, let's just say that she had personality issues," he said indignantly.

"Here we go with the 'broad shoulders' crap. And yeah, she had issues alright," I said chuckling, because we both knew Brenda had more issues than *Time* magazine.

"C'mon, dude," he said defensively. "You've got to admit that Brenda was gorgeous. She had all the right attributes that any man would want."

"Yes, I'll admit that," I said. "She was physically attractive, but that personality left a lot to be desired. She was insecure as hell and wouldn't let you out of her sight for anything other than when you went to work. Even then, she'd call you every hour to make sure that you were where you said you were. And don't be out of pocket for more than thirty minutes because she'd blow up your cell until you checked in. Am I lying?"

"No, man." Greg sighed. "You're not. I guess all that's true. I got tired of that checking in crap. I don't care how good any woman looks, I'm a grown ass man and I don't have to report to anybody. You know I tried to end it, but I don't know what it is I do to these women. You know that when I get into them, they get hooked. She couldn't let go and ended up turning into a super-stalker. I think I need to register my suave charm as a lethal weapon."

"Oh, brother," I groaned. "The real lethal weapon was that screwdriver that she used on your car, remember?"

"How can I forget," he said. "I had to replace all four tires and get it repainted because of the scratches she put on it. Can't believe that I had to end up getting a restraining order."

I thought back to the day that Greg told me his next door neighbor just happened to notice her hiding in the bushes in front of his apartment and called the police. Brenda finally got the hint that their relationship was over when the arresting officer politely told her to watch her head as he placed her in the back seat of his squad car.

"Dang, my brother," Greg said. "I know I've made a few mistakes here or there when it comes to women. Being as dashing and debonair as I am, mistakes are bound to happen."

"Whatever, negro," I said, rolling my eyes again. "The only thing dashing about you was that sprint you did. She had you out there looking like Usain Bolt when she chased you down with that butcher's knife that one time that she thought you were cheating on her. You remember that, right? And speaking of the future, when does her crazy ass get out of jail?"

"I don't know, but whenever she does get out, I'm packing up and moving to Iraq. I heard good things about the women over there."

"Yeah. Right, bruh," I said, laughing. "You talking about running to Iraq, Iran, Bigbuttistan, or wherever else Delta can take you, but the fact is that ever since your divorce from Charlene, you've made horrible choices when it comes to women. Remember Dari? What about Candice? And let's not even talk about Tabitha and her crazy sister. Remember what they did to Magnum?"

"Oh snap. Tabitha," Greg said with a chill in his voice. "Damn shame what they did to that dog."

"See, that's exactly what I'm talking about," I said laughing. "There are great women like Stacey out there but you don't give them the time of day for whatever reason. Either because they don't have bodies like the chicks on a cover of *King* magazine or who knows what. It's like you go for the booty over true beauty every time. Next thing I know, you're calling me to hide out at my house for a few days while the psycho chick of the week loses your scent and can't track you anymore."

"Hold up. Hold up," Greg interjected. "I'll admit that Stacey is very attractive. However, if she's all that then why the hell aren't you talking to her? Why haven't you tried to take her off the market? And since you want to bring up divorces, you haven't had anybody serious in your life since you divorced Cherrelle."

"Good question," I said as I kicked a field goal right as time expired to win the game. "Me and Stacey have been friends for what seems like forever. She's been there through all the various chicks including Cherrelle. I've been there through a bunch of the knuckleheads that have run through her life as well. We're friends in all respect of the word. She's got my back and I've got hers. Nothing more, nothing less."

"Mmm hmm," he said in the skeptical tone that he used when he thought I was feeding him a line of BS.

"And the reason I haven't settled down," ignoring him as I continued, "is because I haven't met a woman that doesn't bore me. I can't find a woman that I can be serious with. I do have a few friends, of which Stacey is one of them. We're just friends."

"If you say so. Just friends, right? You're right, Sir. You've got plenty of friends. Even though I might make a few bad decisions with women from time to time, at least I make a decision. Ever since your divorce, you haven't even thought of committing to anybody. You haven't been with the same woman for more than two weeks at a time. Just when I get one chick's name memorized, you have a new one on your arm. That was a lucky win by the way."

I was stunned. I could not believe he said that. Greg was my best friend in the world and his words truly hurt me. The win was in no way lucky and the way he minimized my triumph was disheartening. My victory was the result of me putting together the perfect game plan on offense and executing terrifically on defense.

I put down the video game controller and reflected on the rest of Greg's statement. He was right in that there hadn't been any one particular love interest in my life since Cherrelle and I split up. We were married for less than six years, and even though things started off good, we knew that we built the marriage on a rocky foundation which inevitably caved in on us.

Cherrelle and I were still friendly to each other. We were both blessed to have made two beautiful children—my 12-year-old daughter, Janice, and my 7-year old son, Victor. After the divorce, we were only cordial at best with each other strictly for the sake of the children. As time passed, we adjusted to our new relationship status and it became easier to deal with each other. She has since gotten remarried and moved to Jacksonville with the kids and her new husband.

"Ethan? You there?" I heard Greg say.

"Yeah, man. I'm here," I responded. "I'm about to grab a bite to eat. I'll hit you back in a few."

"Uhh huh," Greg said. "You get quiet when I tell you about yourself. Hit me when you get back. I'll be here practicing for a while. There's no way in hell you should've won that game. You just distracted me by bringing up Brenda. I'm going to get my game tight and cut down on some of my tendencies."

"Aight, dude. I'll holla at you," I said and shut down the system.

Greg was right when he said that all I have in my life were friends. I had women that would come and go at any given moment and sometimes it felt as if they were only there to fill a particular need just for that moment.

I wondered if the problem was with me or with the women that I kept attracting. Was I really afraid of another committed relationship, or was it because the women I was spending my time with lately were just not worth committing to?

I looked at the blank screen of my television for at least thirty minutes thinking about this.

3

Angel

Lying in my queen-sized bed, wrapped in the sheets which still held the fragrance of our lovemaking, I was comfortably enjoying the post orgasmic glow that enveloped my entire being.

"You haven't said anything to Ethan, have you?" I asked my friend.

"Are you serious?" he asked, stopping in his tracks. He was on his way to the bathroom to wash up when I sprang the question on him.

"Of all the things that could be on your mind after the thrashing that I just handed out, you want to ask me about him?" he said incredulously, rubbing his neatly trimmed beard as he studied me.

I looked at him and burst out laughing. My friend was just over six feet tall with dark brown skin and a thick, muscular body that drove me crazy. He carried himself with a confident swagger and had a great sense of humor.

"Thrashing?" I asked, trying to catch my breath. "Don't get me wrong, it was good, but don't think that you did anything special."

"Whatever, Ma," he said, dropping his voice a few octaves and speaking in that sexy way which never failed to get my juices flowing. "You know a bat can't hit a home run by itself, it's the batter. And I damn sure know how to give you the long stroke and go deep with my big stick, right?"

I felt that familiar tingle beginning to develop in that special area whenever he started talking to me in that manner.

He turned around to face me and pointed at his member.

"Now look at this fine specimen of a bat," he said, gesturing to his impressive, semi-flaccid organ which glistened with the remnants of our lovemaking.

"This is that Georgia good wood right here," he continued.

"The bat may be all that," I said, nodding with approval. "I just want you to know that no matter how good you think you might be throwing it, if you don't have someone on the other end with talent to catch it, you're going to strike out every time. Please believe that I know how to catch it and, even better, I throw it back even harder and better than anybody that you've ever had."

I was staring directly into his eyes as I said this and I saw the excitement darken his visage as he took in my words.

He then rolled his eyes and started laughing.

"That doesn't even make any damn sense. I'm talking about a bat and you talking about a ball. Did you ever play sports?"

"Whatever," I said, joining in his laughter and playfully tossing a pillow at him. "You know what the hell I meant. I'm trying to say that no matter how good you are, having someone who can groove with you makes it even better. Next time don't use a sports analogy and we'll be just fine. Use music or art or something that I'm more familiar with."

"Okay. I'll keep that in mind the next time I give you a good thrashing."

I let my eyes trail down his impressive body. Just looking at him, I felt a tingle run through me as I imagined our next encounter.

He saw where my eyes had settled on his body. In response to my direct stare, his body began to react and his staff started rising and pulsating with excitement.

Of the many things that turned me on about him, the ease with which we could talk to each other about any and everything was by far the biggest turn-on. We used words as aphrodisiacs and they never failed to have us ending up in the nearest bed, backseat, alley, or parking lot. It didn't matter where, as long as we could get a few minutes of privacy, that's all we needed.

The circumstance of us being together was an even more curious situation. We both knew we really didn't have anything to hide, but we decided to keep things as quiet as possible for as long as possible.

"So have you?" I asked, tearing my eyes off his erection and looking at him directly.

The spell broken, he looked at me and started smiling.

"Wow. You're truly relentless," he said with a mixture of awe and mild irritation. "When you've got a question, you want an answer.

Not even the best loving on the planet is going to stop you from getting it. Well, no, I haven't said anything to anybody about us."

I thought about this for a second and let his words settle in my mind.

Ever since our first conversation, we decided that we needed to keep our relationship a secret shared between us. If things went well, then maybe we would be more open with what we had and let everyone know that we were together. If not, we would keep things as they were and continue to enjoy what was a very exciting and mutually fulfilling sexual relationship.

"Have you said anything to her?" he asked.

"No, baby. I haven't said anything to anybody about us either," I answered reassuringly, looking directly into his eyes as I spoke.

He nodded his approval, then turned and continued into the bathroom.

A few seconds later, I heard him brushing his teeth. The reason for him doing so made me recall with a satisfied grin a few other aspects of our earlier activities.

It was getting harder and harder to keep our secret. I was really starting to feel him in ways I never thought I would with any man of his social stature.

He did not own his own home, but was instead renting a small, two-bedroom house. He did have his own car and that was a plus even if it wasn't anything remotely close to the type of high-end luxury automobiles that I was used to.

He was not a member of any fraternal organization, much less having even attended a four-year college. He felt that the whole idea of Greek organizations was silly and had no time for them.

I have been accused of being stuck up because I would not date a man that did not have a college degree, belonged to the right fraternity, owned his own home, and had a net worth of at least five hundred thousand dollars.

I felt I was worth that and a whole lot more, and the man that got with me had to be my equal or better. The problem was that the men who approached me that met these criteria were all the same. They were a boring breed of self-important, corny punks that could barely hold their own penis when they urinated much less handle a real woman such as myself.

The bathroom door opened and he walked back towards the bed. I took in his swagger and felt that familiar tingling sensation which always occurred when I looked at him.

He was not the type of man that I thought I would ever fall for. Lacking a college education had never slowed him down to this point. I had to say that I was impressed when he told me that he had registered to start taking courses in a few months and would be pursuing his ASE certification to become a master mechanic. Little things like that demonstrated the kind of man that he was.

He loved to tinker with cars and worked in one of his friend's garage. With each day, he was developing a solid reputation for doing good, quality work. He had his own repeat customers and would work on their cars in the driveway in front of his house. His customer base was growing so after a while, he decided that he would get his certification and maybe one day open his own shop. He had finally finished his application to attend school and for financial aid and was counting the days until his courses began.

Since the moment we met at a party and began spending time with each other, things with us have always been good. The closer we got with each other, the more he opened up and told me about his past. He didn't reveal too many specifics about his past activities. He did trust me enough to tell me about how those activities caught up to him and resulted in him serving time on an armed robbery sentence. That conviction was how he got the felony record that follows him to this day.

Most of the guys that I had dealt with up to that point barely had speeding tickets on their record, much less a felony of any kind.

He was definitely the antithesis of the kind of man I thought would be my Mr. Right, but he never failed to put a smile on my face with his intellect, sense of humor, passion, and personality.

As he got back into the bed and put his arms around me, I relaxed into his warmth and surrendered into his firm embrace. I loved being in his arms and enjoyed the feeling of security that came when he held me.

As good as my friend made me feel, I feared that we would never be a real couple and would just continue being friends with benefits. I could not get over the nagging thought that we would never overcome the obstacles that lay in the way of us trying to make a go at a real relationship.

4

Stacey

My black Nissan Maxima was parked in the driveway of a gorgeous three-bedroom ranch home in the Lithonia area of metro Atlanta, the first home on the list of potential houses I thought my new client would be interested in purchasing. I was gazing out the window while enjoying the last few sips of my venti cup of Starbucks coffee. It was early in September and fall was just around the corner. The sky was a clear blue and there was not a cloud in sight.

There was a slight breeze which made the mild morning air even that much more pleasant. I had the feeling that today was going to be a good day.

I received a call from Ethan who told me that he had a friend who was looking to purchase a home. Ethan was his regular silly self as he told me about his buddy, Walter, and gave me his phone number.

I knew Walter only by name. He and Ethan were good friends and Ethan had mentioned him to me before, but today would be my first opportunity to meet him in person.

After giving Walter a call, we did a quick phone interview to get the preliminary information I would need as far as his price range, the type of home he would be interested in purchasing, and the area of town he would prefer to live.

Armed with this information, I searched the database of available listings, found the homes that met his criteria, and set up a few showings for him.

As I sat there waiting, I flashed back to my date the night before. I thought about how the evening had started off badly and quickly went downhill with each passing minute.

The voices on the radio broke through my thoughts and caught my attention. Focusing on the host, I listened as he spoke.

"Ladies, you have more power and control over things than you give yourselves credit for," the stand-up comedian turned author and talk-show host was saying in his trademark drawl.

"If y'all allow foolishness, then foolishness is what y'all will get. If you demand the best, then you'll only get the best. You need to know exactly what it is you want, and then accept nothing less than that.

"Now I want y'all to listen closely to this. Y'all need to learn your roles in the relationship with your man. Some of y'all be all up in the driver's seat, telling your man that he better get his behind in the passenger seat 'cause you are an 'independent' woman and you don't need no man telling you nothing. I'll tell you right now, ain't no real man gonna put up with that foolishness for long.

"And some of y'all settle for the back seat in the relationship. Just happy to even be in the car and merrily going along for the ride with a big Kool-Aid grin all on your face. Go when he say go. Do what he say do. Just happy to have somebody there driving.

"Ladies, your role is to be in the passenger seat next to your man, helping him to navigate. Y'all should be working beside each other to get down the tricky roads of this thing we call life. Together."

After listening to these words of wisdom, I clicked off the radio and allowed my mind to drift as I meditated on what was said.

Do I know what I want?

My thoughts were interrupted when a sleek, gray Dodge Challenger pulled up next to me.

I glanced at the clock and saw that he was right on time—9:30 sharp. That was definitely a good sign.

Not bad, I thought. This day might turn out pretty good after all. I can show the four houses on my list and still have the rest of my Saturday to run the few errands I needed to take care of.

I took a quick glance in the rear-view mirror to make sure my hair and make-up were in order and proceeded to get out of my car to go and meet my new client.

I watched him get out of his car and was very impressed with what I saw. He was a little over six feet tall and dressed casually in loose fitting, light blue jeans, a powder blue golf shirt, and Nike running shoes.

As he got closer, I saw that he possessed the physique that I found extremely attractive. He had walnut brown skin and was powerfully built with a thick chest and solid legs. What made my breath catch, however, were his arms. I loved a man with large, developed arms.

The way his shirt was stretched around his muscular biceps, it took all of my self-control not to reach out and rub them.

He smiled warmly at me as he walked over with a confident stride to introduce himself.

"Hello, I'm Walter. Walter Johnson," he said, extended his hand in greeting. "You're Stacey, right?"

"Yes," I said, taking his hand. "Stacey Twiggs. Very nice to finally meet you in person." I tried to keep my smile from turning into a grin. "I put together a few houses that I think you might be interested in. Hopefully one of them will be to your liking."

I wanted to stick to business, hoping that would keep my mind from wandering to places that I did not want it to go.

"Sounds good," he said, turning to look at the house in front of us. "This looks like a great start. Nice neighborhood too. I was checking out the other houses in the area on my way here. Very nice."

Very nice indeed, I thought as I stole another look at Walter. He had a handsome, full face with a neatly trimmed mustache and a warm smile. I knew from our phone interview that he was single, no children, and had a decent income. Straight men with those qualities in Atlanta were few and far between.

"Let me get the key from the lockbox and we can head on in," I said.

We spent the next few hours visiting several houses. The list that I had compiled for him included a ranch style house and two split-level houses. Out of all of them, it was a split-level townhouse that he absolutely fell in love with the minute we entered the foyer.

As he walked through each room, he gushed that it was exactly what he was looking for. It fit his style and more importantly his budget, and he wanted it. He said that was the house for him, no questions and he was ready to make an offer.

I loved his enthusiasm and told him that all he would have to do is fill out the loan application and submit the necessary documentation to get the ball rolling.

"No problem," he said. "I brought all the paperwork you told me to bring. Do I need to wait until Monday to fill out the application? I talked to Ethan and he told me that you don't usually do showings on Saturdays. He said you were doing this as a favor to him."

"Is that what he told you?" I asked, smiling at Ethan's crazy behind for telling him that nonsense. To be so sensible and determined in his business endeavors, Ethan had to have the silliest sense of humor of anyone that I knew.

"I don't know why he told you that," I said. "I do in fact show homes on Saturdays. I did move you to the front of the line since you're his friend though. I think he might have embellished just a little."

"Yeah, that's what it sounds like," Walter said, shaking his head. "Regardless, I'm glad you did move me up though," he continued while taking a long look at me.

I could feel myself blushing and turned my head to hide my embarrassment.

"So...umm...as for the paperwork," I said quickly, trying to regain my composure. "We can head somewhere nearby and fill them out. It shouldn't take but maybe twenty or thirty minutes. I've pretty much gotten everything we'll need to go through the process. We should be able to have everything knocked out in no time."

"Sounds great," he said happily. "There are quite a few restaurants not too far from here. There's a Chili's, Applebee's, IHOP, and a few others. Would that be okay?"

"Sure," I said. "Applebee's would be perfect. I love their fried chicken salad,"

"Cool," he said. "Let's head over there. I've got to make a quick stop on the way and I'll meet you there."

"No problem," I said. "I'll go and get us a table. I'll see you in a few."

I watched as he walked to his car and drove away. I slowly fanned myself as I reached for my cell phone.

I dialed Angel's number and listened as it rang through to her voicemail.

"GIRRRLLLL," I squealed into the phone. "I just showed houses to this foine hunk of a man. I'm about to go meet him for lunch. I'll call you when we finish up. Talk to you later. And I'm still mad at you, heffa. Bye."

I pushed the END key and took a few seconds to read the various text and email messages that were in my inbox.

After that task was complete, I delayed a few more minutes before heading towards the restaurant to meet Walter. I did not want to seem too anxious, nor did I want to walk in there at the same time he did.

5

Walter

I could hardly wait to call Ethan. I was pulling up his number in my cell phone as soon as I backed out of the driveway of what would soon be my new home.

I was in awe of Stacey. No ifs, ands, or buts. She was absolutely gorgeous, both inside and out.

When I initially spoke to her on the phone, I was struck by her voice. It was warm and friendly, yet extremely sensuous without being overtly sexy. At the same time, she handled her business, answering all of my questions thoroughly and professionally with obvious expertise in her field.

I was blown away by her the minute that we met in person. I was so mesmerized that I was damn near speechless. She carried herself with grace and dignity that let you know she was not a person to be taken lightly.

She wore very light make-up which was expertly applied. Unlike a lot of women that I ran across who felt that make-up was there to do just that, make them up into something that they were not, Stacey used her make-up to accent her already very attractive face.

I couldn't understand why my friend for almost the better part of fifteen years had not told me about her. I know Ethan clowns around just about all the time, but Stacey was truly no joke.

His favorite digs are usually at my expense and from the time we met, he has been giving me grief about my size. In high school, I was already a naturally big guy and had just started getting into weight training. Even though I was physically large and naturally strong, I had no real desire to play sports. I reluctantly played football in my sophomore and junior years, and it turned out, I was a pretty good athlete. The issue was that I just never developed any real enthusiasm for the sport and eventually left it alone entirely for my senior year. This was to the chagrin of the head coach who knew that I was the answer to his State Championship dreams. After that, I concentrated on hitting the books and focused my energy on weight training and body building.

I met Ethan when I took a part-time job working at McDonald's on the weekends around the end of my junior year. Ethan, who is a year older than me, was already working there. On my first day on the job, the shift manager escorted me into the grill area to introduce me to the crew. Upon seeing me, Ethan looked me up and down before finally saying in a loud voice, "Looky here Hulk, we don't care what science lab your big muscle-bound ass escaped from. We don't want you to get mad and start throwing the grill around during a busy rush period. I know that we won't like you when you get angry and all that, so just keep all them muscles in check, and we gonna be alright back here. Cool?"

His comment caused the rest of the crew, all of whom had been standing around listening to him, to burst into laughter. Sadly, Ethan and I have been friends ever since.

He took me under his wing and personally trained me for that job, and has been a big brother and friend to me ever since. That didn't mean that he let up any on the teasing. If anything, he has gotten even better and more creative over the years.

"Damn, man," I said as soon as Ethan answered the phone. "Why didn't you tell me?" I asked, trying unsuccessfully to contain my excitement.

"Big Swole?" I heard him saying with a tone of exaggerated calmness. "What in the hell are you talking about? Why didn't I tell you what? Did you drop another barbell on your head? You been inhaling that weight room air again?"

"I'm talking about Stacey, Ethan," I said, ignoring his comments.

"Look, man, I still don't know what you're talking abou...Oh God," he gasped in mock horror. "Did you have another 'roid rage episode, lose control and pummel her to death?"

"Man, you know I don't use steroids," I answered hotly. "And she's just fine. I mean that literally. In fact, that woman is beautiful. That's why I'm calling your ignorant ass. Why didn't you tell me she was so damned sexy?"

"First of all, man," he said. "I didn't think it was relevant as to how she looked, be it butt ugly or beautiful. Your Conan the Barbarian looking behind said you wanted a house. Being that she's a close friend and the real estate agent that helped me get my place, she's obviously the first person that came to mind. That's why I referred you to her.

"Also," he continued, "you could've met her on several occasions before today. There have been so many events, parties, and activities that she was in attendance but you, my muscle bound friend, were nowhere to be seen. Why weren't you there? Well that brings me to my third and final point, and that's Darlene. You haven't forgotten all about that succubus that you call your girlfriend, have you?"

His question quickly sobered me and brought me back to a sad reality that I realized I did not want to face.

"Walterrr, are you still there?" he said in a mocking sing-song voice. "I'm trying to figure out why you're still with that self-centered vulture of a woman. Now look at you. You feel trapped. Check that, you are trapped. Darlene has you by your steroid shrunken balls and now that you've met a real woman like Stacey, you want to call me like I did something wrong. Not going work, dude."

I wanted to respond to Ethan and tell him how wrong he was. I wanted to tell him that I wasn't trapped at all. I wanted to tell him that I was happily in love. I wanted to tell him all of those things but I couldn't. He knew the truth. I knew the truth.

"Walt?" I heard Ethan saying. "You there, homie?" he asked, taking a more serious tone. "Look, man. I know the real deal with you and Darlene. I know that in your heart, you really don't love her. Even if you can't or don't want to say it, I know the truth. I've also known Stacey for a long time and I know that she's a great woman. Real talk, Walter, you aren't ready for a woman like her or anybody else until you get your situation with Darlene straight. You know what you need to do. Just find it within yourself to do it. Whatever you do though, just know I got your back, okay?"

I held the phone to my ear and listened to my friend's words and knew that he spoke the truth. I knew what I needed to do, and I knew that it had to be done sooner rather than later.

"I know, man," I said quietly. "Thanks, dude. I appreciate you being there for me."

"No prob, Herc," he said, laughing.

"Whatever man," I said, starting to laugh myself. "Your flabby butt's just jealous of my body, so stop hating."

"Nice try, Walt," he said. "You've got absolutely nothing that I would want to be jealous of. Anyway, are you finished looking at houses already?"

"Yeah, we're through. I found one that I like, too," I answered, putting on my signal to turn into the approaching parking lot. "In fact, I'm about to head up into Applebee's to meet Stacey to take care of some paperwork. She's on her way here now."

"Hold up. Y'all are going to Applebee's? Like on a date?" Ethan asked in surprise.

"No. Well, not really. Look, man, I just got here. I gotta go. I'll hit you later," I said and hit the END button, cutting Ethan off before he could say anything else.

6

Stacey

We had spent the last hour and a half going over everything that Walter would need to purchase his home. Completing our business, he and I laughed and talked as we enjoyed the remainder of our meal together. I was surprised at how the afternoon had turned out and especially how easily the conversation between us was going. I had anticipated taking maybe thirty minutes at most for us to go over everything, but here we were, well into our second hour, enjoying each other's company.

"That was delicious. I tried to make something like this at home but mine wasn't even close to being this good," I said, commenting on my entrée of grilled salmon with garlic and herbs.

"Yeah, right," Walter said with a skeptical tone. "I'm sure you're a great cook. You're just trying to be modest. I bet you're like Sunny Anderson in the kitchen."

"Not even close," I responded with a smile. "Don't get me wrong, though. I'm not going to brag and say that I'm all that but I can throw a few things together."

"Oh, really? Well I tell you what," Walter said. He took the last bite of his grilled chicken, wiped his mouth with his napkin, and looked directly into my eyes. "How about you cook for me sometime? Maybe after I close on the house, you could come by one day and help me break in the kitchen?"

I was surprised by his questions and took a sip of my water while I thought about it.

It had been so long since I had met a man as attractive and interesting as Walter. For the longest, it was like I was the Red Cross of the dating game. I only seemed to get the sick, diseased, or the infirmed that wanted to get with me.

I knew my worth and what I would bring to the table in a relationship. I did not know why I could not seem to find the right man for me.

I did not consider myself in the ranks of women who felt they needed a man in order to feel relevant. Since the death of my husband, Stephen, more than a decade ago, I have been through so many changes in order to get to where I was. In fact, I was comfortable with my life as it was and had no problem living out the rest of my days with just my daughter and my dog.

Stephen's death scared me to my core. One day you have a happy, complete family and in the blink of an eye, your whole world crumbles around you.

I wasn't looking for a man to replace Stephen, but I wanted someone that could be my friend and companion. The few dates that

I had been on to this point held no promise to fill either of these desires.

Sitting with Walter, I could definitely feel something. I felt a tingle of excitement that I had not felt with any man since Stephen. This feeling both scared and fascinated me.

Gathering myself, I had to make sure that I did not allow my emotions to take over my common sense.

After taking another sip of my water, I took a deep breath and said, "That actually does sound like a good idea. I usually make it a point not to date my clients. I prefer to keep my personal and professional lives as far apart as possible. That being said, I wouldn't mind taking you up on your offer for dinner. But that's if and when we got to know each other better. I don't know anything about you, and you don't know anything about me."

He sat back in his chair and closed his eyes as he absorbed my words. Finally, he opened them and looked at me.

"I only know the basics about you," I continued. "I know that you aren't married but that's not the same as being single. I will not even think about talking to a man that's already in a relationship. I'm too grown to be anybody's side chick so if that's what you're looking for, you might as well keep it moving."

"No, that's definitely not what I'm looking for. And you're right," he said quietly. "You don't know much about me at all. I'd like to get to know you better and for you to get to know me as well. I'm going to be honest with you. There is someone in my life. The situation's not a good one and has been that way for a long time. I didn't realize just how bad it was until today. I know that I've got to take care of things and do something that I should've done a long time ago."

The silence that hung in the air after Walter finished speaking was mercifully interrupted by our server as she came to remove our plates.

"Would you guys care for dessert?" she asked cheerfully.

"No, thank you," we both said in unison.

"We'll take the check, please," I said.

"I'll take care of it," Walter offered.

"No, you're my client after all, so I'll handle it. This time," I said.

"This time?" he asked in surprise. His entire demeanor changed and a huge smile spread across his face.

"Yes, this time. Next time depends on what you do or don't do. We shall see," I said as I reached into my purse and pulled out my credit card, making sure to avoid making eye contact with him as I did so.

I wondered if I was making the right move or if it was a huge mistake to not nipping whatever this was in the bud. I have heard that line before from several guys that I had dealt with in the past.

"Yeah, baby. Me and my wife are separated," or "We're just roommates," and any number of lies in between. Usually the minute I hear those words, I get my things and walk out the door without looking back, immediately block their number, and move on.

With Walter, there was something different. I couldn't put my finger on what it was that made me feel that way. Maybe it was our conversation or the honest way that he told me about his situation. I hoped that it wouldn't come back and bite me but I did not want to close the door on him. I would keep it professional, of course, but I also would not eliminate anything else that might be.

7

Ethan

I was lounging on my couch, flipping between the channels that were showing the many college football games on the day's schedule. My mind was replaying the conversation I had with Walter a few hours ago and also my conversation with Greg yesterday.

As I watched the flickering images on the screen and heard the commentators drone on about the action on the field, I could not get my mind to focus on anything in particular.

Walter was a punk when it came to Darlene. Now that he had met a very special woman in Stacey, he was stuck between a rock and a mental case. I had no love for Darlene and had never hidden that fact. She was a she-devil who was sucking the life out of my boy and barely giving him anything in return. I knew that Walter was only hurting himself for staying in that situation for as long as he had, but that didn't change the fact that at least he had a situation to stay in.

Greg was a player to the end. He had more women running behind him than he could sometimes keep up with. Every other night it seemed, he was talking about getting with one chick or the other.

The longest relationship I could remember him being in was with his ex-wife and even then, he had other women on the side.

I loved my boys but after reviewing their different situations, I could not help but be left with a feeling of jealousy towards them.

They had somebody and I did not. That was the bottom line. There was no ~~way~~ other way around it.

I thought I had grown comfortable in my bachelorhood. I had two beautiful, healthy children. I had a nice home. I had all the toys I wanted. I owned a successful business. I had it all. Or so it seemed. I wanted more. I needed more. I wanted an exclusive, special woman.

Picking up my phone from the armrest of the couch scrolling through the address book, I reviewed all the names in my contact list. I shook my head in both disbelief and disgust. There were several who would be great situations for the night; however there were absolutely no good long term prospects.

A jolt of excitement hit me when I came across one particular name and number. Looking at the entry of 'Monica Nolastname', I thought back to when I met Ms. Monica. I sat back in my chair and looked up at the ceiling, losing myself in the memory of that weekend.

I was attending the Black Business Owners Convention, which was being held in Seattle, Washington of all places. As the owner of a small, minority-owned business, I made it a point to try and attend as many of these conventions and conferences as possible, even if they happened to be on the other side of the country. The networking aspect was incredible as I had made several invaluable contacts throughout the years. Another benefit was that since I loved to travel, I was able to visit different cities each year and write off each trip as a legal business expense.

I had a room at the Silver Cloud Hotel in downtown Seattle. My room overlooked the Kingdome, the home of the Seattle Mariners baseball team, and I had a great view of the infield. I'm not a big baseball fan, but to be able to look across the street and see the lush, manicured green grass of the stadium was a real treat for me.

It was a Friday afternoon and I had just left the convention center to go back to my room to relax for a while. I read over a few of the brochures and other sales materials that I had collected from some of the vendors earlier in the day before deciding to head down to the hotel lounge to enjoy a drink and engage in one of my favorite activities—people watching.

As soon as I walked into the lounge, I saw her. She was sitting at the bar and it was almost as if there was a spotlight shining on her. She was an incredibly gorgeous woman, thick with plenty of breasts, built just the way I liked. I collected myself and walked over to where she was seated.

I could not decide on what opening to use or just how to approach her, but I knew that someway, somehow, I was going to speak to this beautiful creature.

Once I got to the bar and was standing a few seats away from her, I smiled to myself as soon as I saw my opening present itself.

I got the bartender's attention and ordered my favorite drink, a Cîroc Coconut and Coke. As the bartender prepared it, I waited a few minutes before casually turning and pointing to the concoction in the glass in front of her.

"Excuse me, Miss," I said in my most polite tone, "I don't want to disturb you, but I've got to ask. What is that? I don't think I've ever seen anything like it."

She turned, looked at me, and gave me the most radiant smile.

"I'm still trying to figure it out," she said, shaking her head. "Let me rephrase. I know what it is; I just don't know why I ordered it."

"Now that makes more sense," I said, chuckling.

"It's a bacon martini," she added. "It has hot sauce, bacon vodka, and real bacon bits. It sounded good, so I decided to try it."

"So you're a risk taker? The adventurous type?" I asked, taking my drink from the bartender and moving closer to her.

"I can be at times. I'm in a new city, so I figured, why not try something new?" she said as she drank some of the mixture.

She wrinkled her nose and frowned deeply, a mild shudder overcoming her before she forced the liquid down with an audible gulp.

The bartender, who had been quietly watching her drink, started laughing at her reaction. "You're the seventh person who's ordered that drink in the four months since it's been on the menu, and the reaction is always the same. Nobody likes it. The only reason we even put it on the menu is because our liquor supplier gives us discounts on other products that we buy from them."

I took a sip of my drink and said, "I'll just stick to what I know. I'm not as courageous as this young lady here." I nodded at my new friend. "Would you like something a little bit tamer, or are you going to keep soldiering through the pain and finish that one?"

"Nope! I'm done. I'm tapping out," she said, shaking her head vigorously and hitting her palm on the bar. "I'll have a chocolate martini, please. And can you please take this thing back," she said to the bartender.

"Sure thing. Be right back," the bartender replied as he took the drink away.

Scanning the room, I noticed that a secluded table in the back had opened up.

"Can you bring that to us when it's ready, please? We'll be right over there," I told the bartender, motioning to the table.

"No problem," he responded.

"Kind of bold, aren't you?" she said, trying to give me a stern look, but the smile playing at the corners of her mouth told me that I had made the right move.

"As a matter of fact, yes. I'm very determined by nature. In this case though, I wouldn't call it being bold. I'd say it's more like being proactive," I said, standing up and bending my arm, indicating for her to take it.

She paused for a second before standing and putting her arm in the crook of my offered arm and walking with me to the empty table.

As I pulled out a chair and held it for her, I took the opportunity to give her the once over. I was thoroughly impressed with her physical appearance. She was wearing a colorful yellow and blue sundress that showcased her sexy figure and complimented her smooth dark caramel complexion. With full breasts and a more than ample behind attached to a pair of thick thighs, her hair was pulled back into a tight bun that was just perfect for her round face. An intelligent pair of light brown eyes sat behind her small, rectangular framed glasses which were perched on a cute button nose.

"Why thank you. Bold and a gentleman. Very nice," she commented as she sat down.

"My dad taught me right," I said, walking around the table and taking the seat across from her.

"I see," she said, looking at me thoughtfully. "I hope he also taught you how to introduce yourself, or did you just forget that lesson? I don't even know your name. I don't usually take drinks and sit with total strangers but as I said, I'm being a bit of a risk taker today."

"I'm sorry," I said, slapping my palm to my forehead. "I completely forgot. I'm sitting over here mentally kicking myself for forgetting your name so quickly that I forgot to tell you mine."

I stood and extended my hand across the table to her and said, "My name is Ethan. Ethan Lucas."

"Very nice to meet you, Ethan," she replied, taking my extended hand and giving it a firm, yet feminine shake. "And the reason why you can't remember mine is because I didn't tell you. It's Monica."

"Just Monica? No last name?" I asked, reluctantly releasing her hand before sitting back down.

"For now, it's just Monica. Like Prince. Or Tamia," she said with a wink.

The bartender brought her drink over and we talked for what seemed like hours on a wide range of topics. I learned that she was in town for a baking seminar and was staying at a hotel a few blocks away from mine. Being the owner of a bakery that specialized in baked goods and confections infused with alcohol, she explained that was one of reasons she decided to give the bacon vodka martini a try.

At several points in the evening, her cell phone rang, interrupting the conversation. Each time, she took it out her purse, looked at the caller-ID screen, and frowned at the display while shaking her head.

On the fifth time of her ringing phone interrupting us, I could not contain myself any longer.

"Is everything okay?" I asked.

"Oh, yes. I'm sorry. Everything's fine. I just have some crazy things going on back home. I thought I'd be able to get away from them for a while but that just doesn't seem to be the case," she said, turning away from me, but not before I was able to see the expression of sadness that had come across her face.

"You know what?" she said, suddenly rising to her feet. "I've got to go. I completely lost track of time. I've got to head back to my hotel."

I stood up with her and reached out, putting my hand on her arm as she gathered up her things.

"Are you sure everything's okay? I can walk there with you, if you like," I offered. I was being sincere; however, I still wanted any opportunity to spend a few more minutes with her.

"Thank you but I'm going to catch a cab," she said before reaching into her purse and giving me one of her business cards.

I took it and reflexively reached into my pocket to give her one of mine.

"Thank you for a wonderful evening, Ethan. It was a pleasure meeting you," she said as she took the card. She then gave me a quick kiss on the cheek and headed out of the room and towards the hotel's front door.

I stood in silence for a few moments, trying to figure out what had happened. I slowly sat back down in my chair and looked at her card clenched in my hand. I read the information about her business—Sweet Sinsations, a bakery specializing in alcohol infused cakes and desserts—and smiled at the catchy name. Her card only had the contact information for the business, which was located in New Orleans, and her first name, Monica, with no last name given. I crumpled it up and tossed it on the table in frustration.

I stared at the rumpled card for a few minutes before I picked it up and smoothed it out. *You never know what the future holds*, I said to myself as I took out my cell phone and programmed her name and number into the device's address book.

I might as well call her, I thought now, all these many months later as I looked at her name in my phone.

What could it hurt? At best, she would remember me; at worst, she wouldn't. No harm, no foul.

I finally made the decision and had just moved my thumb to the CALL button right as the doorbell rang, announcing the delivery guy had arrived with my order of pizza and hot wings.

I'll call her later, I thought as I tossed the phone aside and went to answer the door.

8

Walter

*O*f all the places that I could be on a Sunday afternoon during football season, a women's shoe store in the mall was most definitely not high on that list. I was sitting in an uncomfortable chair in the fifth shoe store that we had visited today on our day-long excursion to Stonecrest Mall.

Earlier, Darlene had been hit with the whim to go shoe shopping and, as usual, I was dragged along. It seemed like her sudden itches only needed to be scratched right when I was in the middle of doing something I enjoyed, and therefore, was not giving her my undivided attention.

Just a few short hours ago, I was in full couch potato mode, enjoying my Sunday afternoon, watching the day's spate of NFL games. Flipping between the Eagles/Cowboys game on Fox and the Steelers/Browns game on CBS, I was thoroughly relaxed with my feet propped up on the coffee table. I was comfortably lounging, munching on Doritos and washing them down with a big cup of my special blend of orange and lemon-lime Kool-Aid. It was at that moment when Darlene came into the living room, turned off the television, and told me to get dressed because I was going to go shopping with her.

She didn't wait for a commercial break before she turned off the television. She didn't ask me if I had other plans for the day. She didn't ask me if I wanted to go shopping. Nope. She just told me that I was going to go with her and that was the end of it.

"Darlene, I don't want to go shopping. I don't want to go anywhere. I'm going to stay right here on this couch and watch football," I said as I picked up the remote and clicked the television back on.

"You're going to do no such thing," she responded and turned the television right back off. She gave me the same look a parent would give a disobedient child, before turning and leaving the room.

I was in no mood for another argument, so I said the hell with it. I went into the bedroom and took my time getting dressed as I reluctantly put on a pair of jeans and my favorite pair of Timberlands.

Her behavior was typical Darlene. Right about now, I was tired of it. I was sick of the lack of respect, if any at all, that she showed me. I made it a point to not speak to her the entire drive to the mall. I continued the silent treatment as we went from store to store.

"So which pair do you like?" Darlene asked for the third time. She was holding up two pair of suede, high heel ankle boots, one red and the other black.

"Walter? Are you listening to me?" she snapped, her voice sharp, cutting through my thoughts, her angry tone demanding that I speak to her.

"Yes, Darlene." I sighed, her every word grating on my nerves like cheese through a shredder. "I'm listening to you," I said in exasperation. I took a quick look at each shoe before answering her. "The red ones, okay. I like the red ones."

"The red ones? You like those?" Darlene asked, frowning with disapproval. "I think you like the black ones. No, you're wrong about the red ones. I'm going to get the black ones," she said, nodding with satisfaction as she turned to go to the register to purchase them.

"If I liked the black ones I would've said that," I snapped, my frustration with her transforming into anger. "Why the hell did you ask for my opinion if you're going to tell me what I supposedly like?"

Darlene stopped in her tracks and turned to look at me. She held on her face an expression that was both a mixture of shock and disbelief.

"Walter, I don't know what's going on with you," she said, staring directly at me and saying each word in the measured tone that she only used when she was trying to contain her anger. Sadly, I knew that tone all too well. "Ever since you got home yesterday, you've been acting completely different. You're acting like you don't want to be here with me. You've been distracted and haven't been paying any attention to me. If you're still upset with me for not going with you yesterday, then so be it, but don't ever talk to me like that again. I don't know what's gotten into you, but I don't like it."

I started to respond but instead I just blew out my breath in a loud exhalation of frustration and made my way to the exit. I said nothing as I walked by her, and I could feel her stare piercing daggers into my back as I left.

I was in the upper corridor of the mall, leaning over the railing, looking at the throngs of people below going in and out of the stores on the lower level. As I processed how things had fallen into place this weekend, I was really glad that Darlene had not come with me yesterday like I had asked her several times to do. She said that she wanted to move out of Lithonia and could not understand why I was looking at homes in the area. So, like we always did, instead of going with me, she went out with her girlfriends instead.

My mind was consumed with thoughts of Stacey, our lunch meeting, and how the few hours I spent with her had made such a huge impact on me. I could not get her out of my mind. The more I thought about her, the more I knew that it was time for me to make the move that I should have done a long time ago.

I was so tired of Darlene's selfish ways. I was not happy with her and had not been for a long time. The sad truth was that I just did not love her. In fact, in those quiet moments when I'm being honest with myself, I did not even like her. Sadly, I'd felt this way for a long time but did not want to face the truth that I was in a long-term relationship with someone that I did not like. That thought made me sick to my stomach. I had to do something about my situation and it had to be done in a hurry.

I met Darlene Quarry about three years ago after She had recently graduated from Texas Southern University in Houston. Once she completed her master's degree in computer network engineering, she moved to Atlanta. She had only been in the area for over a year when we met. I had just started working at the Sports Rehab Center of Atlanta and she was a member of the team of technicians who were installing a new data network and upgrading our computer system at the clinic.

Where I have always been somewhat reserved and soft spoken, Darlene is the complete polar opposite of me starting from the first day that we met. I was coming out of one of the training rooms when I literally bumped into her. She took a step back to gather herself, looked me up and down, and basically told me that we were going to go out that upcoming Friday. I was so thrown by her assertiveness that all I could do was silently nod in agreement.

The next thing I knew, we went out on our first date, which turned into ten, which turned into us being a couple.

To this day, our entire relationship was a blur to me. She sets the tone and dictates what we are doing, when we are doing it, and how long it will be done. I've lost track of the amount of times that I wanted to go to her and tell her that she and I were over, but for some reason, I could not do it.

Darlene is a very attractive woman with a lean, toned body. Her most striking features are her piercing brown eyes. That plus her smooth, brown skin, full lips, and firm breasts never failed to arouse me. There was definitely no lack of physical attraction towards her but the lack of an emotional connection had taken its toll on me.

Regardless of me feeling this way about her, I still didn't know what kind of spell or hold she had on me, and I didn't know what I could do to get out from under it.

As I stood there with those thoughts running through my mind, I felt her come up behind me. I could feel the heat of the anger coming from her which made me turn to face her.

She looked at me, eyes narrowed into slits, and said nothing as she dropped the bags containing her purchases, one of which I was sure probably contained her new black high heels, at my feet.

We stood there looking at each other for what felt like hours before I bent down to pick up the bags.

"We need to talk," I hissed through clenched teeth.

I turned and started walking towards the food court without another word. I did not look back to see if she was following me and honestly did not care one way or the other if she was.

I got to the food court in the center of the mall and looked around, trying to find an available table. I wanted to talk to her in a more private setting but didn't want to put off what I had to say to her any longer. There would be no waiting until we got back to the apartment to get this done.

I found a table towards the back that was about as isolated as it got in a mall food court. Pulling out one of the chairs, I placed Darlene's bags down and then pulled out a seat for myself.

As I sat, I closed my eyes and took a deep breath in an attempt to calm my nerves. I was so upset with Darlene and her selfish behavior but the truth was, I was upset with myself.

I had nobody to blame for how things were, and it was time for me to do something about it.

Darlene walked up to the table and took a seat. She silently looked at me, her arms crossed over her chest as she angrily waited on me to speak.

I said a silent prayer and then gathered myself to speak the words that had been sitting on my heart for a long time.

"Darlene, I can't do this anymore," I said, getting straight to the point so that I would not lose my courage and go back on my decision.

Once I got that out, it was like a dam burst within me as the words that I have been wanting to say for so long came spilling out.

"I'm not happy with this relationship. I'm not happy with you. I'm not happy with myself. I need to make some changes in my life and the first will be this relationship. There's no more us, Darlene."

She sat and stared at me in silence for a few minutes. I could see the changing emotions across her face as she digested my words.

"I...I...I," she stammered, her eyes wide with shock. "I don't know what to say," she finally said after collecting herself.

She closed her eyes and was quiet for a moment.

"How long have your felt this way?" she asked quietly, her eyes still remaining closed.

"For a long time," I answered softly.

Her eyes flew open wide, her body flinching as if she had been physically struck by my words.

I turned away from her, not being able to look at her directly, and continued in a quieter tone. "I'm sorry to spring this on you like this, but I never knew how to tell you. You know I don't like to argue or fuss, so I just kept my feelings inside and tried to convince myself that I really was happy and everything would just work itself out."

"I see. And here I am thinking that one day we might get married but instead, you are trying to break up with me?" she asked.

I took a second to gather my thoughts, curious as to what she meant by 'trying' to break up with her. I thought that was exactly what I was doing. I was momentarily distracted when an attractive young woman with two small children came over to the table beside us and sat down. She was juggling her shopping bags along with a tray filled with slices of pizza and cups of soda. She dropped her bags by her seat and put down the tray of food on the table. Giving us a weary yet friendly smile, she began to get her children settled down to eat.

The kids—a boy who looked to be around four and his little sister, who just moments ago were bouncing around with unbridled energy, were now quiet with anticipation as their mother put a slice of the hot pizza and a cup in front of them.

The young mother took this time of momentary peace to sit back and relax. She nibbled on a muffin while sipping on a cup of coffee as she looked lovingly at her kids as they messily devoured their meal.

I studied this scene with fascination. As I observed the mother and her family, the reality hit me that I would never have anything remotely close to that with Darlene.

"We won't be getting married, Darlene," I answered, refocusing my thoughts on the matter at hand, knowing that I had to finish the conversation with Darlene.

"In fact, can we go outside?" I asked, pointing through the window behind us to a small bench outside by the mall's entrance.

"That's fine," she snapped and started to gather up her packages.

"I'll get those for you," I said instinctively and started reaching for the bags.

"No! I can get them myself," she said loudly.

The force and volume of her words caused the woman and her children to stop eating and look at us. She smiled uncomfortably at us before telling her children to finish eating.

"Okay, Darlene," I said with my arms upraised in a surrender. "Get them yourself. I was just trying to help. I'll hold the door for you if that's okay."

We walked to the door that led outside which I held open for her. I then moved around her and went to an unoccupied bench and sat down. Darlene took a seat on the opposite end of the bench and put her bags on the ground by her feet.

The cool, crisp, fresh air outside was a stark contrast to the stale, climate controlled environment we had just left.

Without warning, Darlene looked at me and asked softly, "Do you love me?"

Her question caught me completely off guard, and I had to really think about my answer.

She waited a few seconds and then repeated her question, this time with more strength and conviction. "Do you love me?"

"I...I think so," I lied weakly.

I regretted the words the moment they left my lips.

"You think so?" she boomed, her eyes instantly filling with moisture. "You think so? After all this time, the best you can say is that you 'think' you love me?"

The tears started flowing down her cheeks, making my heart break. A very proud and strong woman, in all of the time that we were together, I had never seen her cry. Even when her mother passed away suddenly last year, Darlene was unemotional and stoic. She held all of her feelings inside of an emotional vault that she didn't open for anyone. That was one of the many problems I had with her. She didn't share any of her feelings with me. Throughout our time together, I felt as if I had never gotten to know the real Darlene and I could never get her to open up to me.

I leaned forward on the bench, looked down at my tan suede boots, and listened to Darlene's soft sobs.

"I do care about you, Darlene," I said finally. "It's just that it's hard to love someone that you really don't know. You never really let me get to know you and you definitely don't know me."

She was quiet for a moment as she sat and looked at me. Finally, she took the Kleenex which she had fished out of her purse and used it to dry her eyes and wipe away her tears.

Once she was fully composed, she methodically gathered her bags and stood up, her back straight.

"What are you doing? Where are you going" I asked, looking up at her in confusion.

"I'm ready to go home," she said coolly. "Are you just going to sit there?"

I was shocked by the change in demeanor. It was like the previous conversation had never even happened. We might as well have been talking about the shoes in her bag or the weather for all of the emotion that she was exhibiting. She had instantly transformed from an emotional human being into a cold, unfeeling robot.

"No. I'm coming," I said, standing to my feet, still confused by her rapid mood swing.

"Good. So what do you want for dinner?" she asked calmly.

Not even waiting for an answer, she turned on her heels and walked towards the parking lot with a confident stride, her hips swaying with each step.

9

Stacey

It was third down and my Saints were looking at a long twelve yards to gain a first down. I just knew they were going to have to punt, but instead Jimmy Graham snatched the perfect Drew Brees' pass out of the air, juked the linebacker that was futilely trying to tackle him, and then turned on the jets.

"Yeaaahh!" I screamed, jumping off the couch in excitement when he not only got the first down, but sprinted towards the end zone for the score, putting my Saints ahead of the Patriots by two scores.

It was a relaxing Sunday and I was watching my favorite football team and enjoying a few glasses of wine. After several long weeks that started on Mondays and went all the way through Saturdays, I had learned to appreciate the downtime that my Sundays offered.

It felt so good to just relax and do nothing but spend time with Brianna. We hadn't spent that much time together and some quality mommy-daughter time was way past due. The past few weeks had been extremely hectic with showings, closings, meetings, endless phone calls, and running from one end of Atlanta to the other. It seemed like everything was coming back-to-back with no break in between. There was no free time left for much beyond sleeping during the week, so a weekend like this where I had nothing scheduled was a treasure to be enjoyed. As much as I loved the increase in business which meant an increase in commissions, I really needed my down time to sit back and unwind.

Just as Graham crossed the goal line and started flexing his muscles to celebrate the touchdown, I heard my cell phone ringing.

"Ugghh. Dammit! Who's calling me now?" I said in frustration as I threw off my Saints Snuggie and ran into the kitchen to get my phone off the charger.

"Hello?" I said while looking back at the television and watching the replay of the touchdown.

"Hey, girl," Angel said, half-screaming into my ear. "What're you doing? You got company over there?"

"Company? Me? Yeah, right." I chuckled, picking up the remote and pushing the pause button on the game.

There was more truth to my response than Angel could realize. I wished I did have someone special on the couch beside me. Even though I was more than comfortable being by myself, having company on a day like today would be wonderful.

"It's just me and Brianna," I said. "I'm downstairs watching the game and Bri's upstairs in her room. I'm all alone over here watching the Saints destroy these sorry Patriots. My boys are really putting it on them and when they win, they'll be on top of the division. I feel another Super Bowl championship coming this year!

"Anyway, I'm missing my game and I know you didn't call to talk football, so what's up?" I asked, trying to hide my impatience at her interruption.

"Not a thing," she said. "I was sitting here trying to finish this book but really couldn't concentrate on it. There isn't anything good on television and I wasn't in the mood to watch football, so I was calling to see what you were up to. I didn't realize the Aints were playing. I know how caught up you get when the game's on."

"Please don't hate, heffa," I said to her. "Just because you and the rest of the fair weather Falcons fans in this city are trying to get rid of their season tickets on e-Bay. Or did you forget that?"

"Whatever," Angel said, laughing. "I just needed some extra cash, that's all. I knew I shouldn't have told you about that."

"You sure shouldn't have," I said. "But seriously, what's going on?"

"Like I said, I really didn't want anything in particular," she said. "I was just calling to see what you were up to. Since you're watching your game, just give me a call later."

I could tell by the tone of her voice that there was a lot on her mind. She always tried to present an upbeat and energetic front but I knew the real Angel. I knew she was a very emotional woman at her core.

"Nah, girl," I said, looking sadly at the TV. The screen was frozen just as the Saints were getting ready to kick off to the Patriots, but I knew that I wouldn't be watching any more of the game any time soon. With a quiet sigh, I clicked the television off as I sat back down on the couch.

"This game's a blow-out anyway. What's on your mind?" I asked.

"Nothing, really. Honestly, I'm feeling a little lonely right now and needed someone to talk to." She sighed.

"Umm, Angel, I'm not sure how to put this, but you're my girl and all, but you're definitely not my type," I said, hearing the pain in her voice and trying to make her smile.

"Whatever, chick!" she said, laughing. "You aren't my type either. You don't have the equipment that I need, thank you!"

Her laughter tapered off and I heard her take a deep breath before she continued.

"I was sitting here thinking about my friend, that's all. I know that I like him, but I can't help but feel like I'm settling for less if I was to pursue something with him. I don't know what to do."

"I don't know either," I said. "Have you talked to him? I mean really talked to him. Told him how you feel? Told him what you want?"

My question caused her to fall silent for a few seconds.

"To be honest," she said finally, "I haven't told him anything. I've hinted that I need more from him a couple of times, but I don't think that he's gotten my hints. I want to tell him but I haven't done so yet."

"Hints? I don't understand. How would he know what you want if you haven't specifically told him?" I asked, genuinely curious of her exact dilemma. I was truly confused as to what she was expecting to happen. She was telling me that she wanted more from her friend; however, she didn't tell him just what her true desires were. Unless he was some kind of a mind reader, he would have a hard time trying to meet her needs and expectations if he didn't know what they were.

"As much time as we've spent together," she said, "I would think that he'd have the same feelings that I do. The real problem is that I want a man that can provide more than just the physical. He and I have a great physical relationship, there's no doubt about that. I want a man that can give me more of the finer things that life has to offer. I believe that I'm worth that and so much more, right?"

"Yes, you're worth all of that and there's nothing wrong with wanting a man to provide those things," I said. "But men really aren't that bright. If you don't tell them exactly what you want and you leave it up to them to try and figure it out on their own, you'll be waiting a long time. If you want something, don't throw hints. You need to tell him. And more importantly, is he even able to provide you with the things that you want? It's usually one or the other. You have to decide what you want now and how long you're willing to wait while he develops the other."

"I know," she said. "Or I can get with a man who already has money in the bank and train him on how to please me physically. That's my dilemma. Either way, you're right. I'll have to tell him exactly what I want. If I don't, then I'll never be happy. Or at least not with him.

"But anyway, thanks for listening to me. I think I need to get something in my stomach. I've been wanting a plate of Jamaican food all week so I might as well get my behind up and go get some," she said in an obvious attempt to mask her sadness with false excitement. "Ox-tails, rice and peas from Island Cafe, here I come!"

"Girl, now you got me hungry. I wasn't even thinking about food and now I'm starving all of a sudden," I said to her. "Go get your grub on. As soon as the game ends, I'm going to see what Bri' wants to eat and then we might head out. Don't worry, Angel," I said reassuringly. "Things will work themselves out. They always do. Just keep praying and trust your heart."

"Thanks, Stacey. I appreciate you listening to me. I'll let you know how it works out," she said and hung up.

I thought about Angel's desires for her ideal man that could both please her physically and still provide her with the lifestyle that she desired. Her wants were a lot different than mine, but at the end of the day, we both longed for one man who could give us all of the things that we felt that we wanted and needed. Once again I thought about having that special someone to be with me.

Maybe one of these days, I thought as I clicked on the television to finish watching the game.

10

Ethan

*A*s I pulled into my parking space and dismounted from my motorcycle, I knew that today was going to be a good day. It was a picture perfect mid-October day with clear skies and a slight breeze blowing gently.

The feeling of pride that came over me every time I walked through the doors of my small trucking company never grew old. Consisting of a fleet of seventeen units, I had a team of twenty-one employees and had a great relationship with each of them. With trucks running all over the Southeast and plans to grow the business by adding more units to the fleet, things were going very well. Growth wasn't as fast as I would have liked; however, I was very thankful for the steady development of my company over the last few years.

I checked the area of the parking lot where the trucks were usually parked and saw that it was empty. This was a good sign as it meant that all the trucks were out somewhere on the road earning revenue.

After looking around the lot for a final time, I headed towards the building. As soon as I walked inside, the first thing I saw was Jerome Thomson's skinny butt damn near laying down on Cassandra Peele's desk. His face was so close to hers that it looked as if I would have walked in a few seconds later, they would have been engaged in a full-fledged, make-out session.

"Ahem!" I said, clearing my throat dramatically.

"Oh shi…" Cassandra, my long-time office manager, said as she pushed Jerome away.

"Mawnin', boss man," he said, quickly hopping off her desk with a big, toothy grin on his face.

"Damn, y'all," I said, shaking my head at their antics. "Every time I turn around, you two are all up in each other's face. Jerome, shouldn't you be out driving somewhere? Cassandra, did you finish up those reports for me?"

"Ethan, stop playing," Cassandra said, trying to hide her embarrassment.

"Get up out of here and leave her alone so she can get some work done. Go check and see how the repairs are going on your truck. If it's ready to go, then you need to roll out."

"No problem, boss," Jerome responded and gave me a pound. "See you later, baby," he said to Cassandra, as he walked by her desk and gave her a mischievous grin before heading out the back door of the office which lead to the shop.

"Bye, boy," Cassandra mumbled through the smile that she tried unsuccessfully to cover up.

As I walked by her desk on the way to my office, I tried to give her the most stern look possible. Instead of shrinking back in shock and fear, she instead stuck her tongue out at me. This caused both of us to burst into laughter.

After getting into my office and settling in behind my desk, I tried to clear my mind and prepare myself for work.

It was almost one in the afternoon when Cassandra knocked on my door to ask about lunch. Her timing could not have been more perfect as the rumbling of my stomach, which I had been trying to ignore for the last half hour, was starting to get louder and louder.

"I was thinking Chinese today," she said.

"Chinese it is," I said in agreement. "I need to use your car though since I rode the bike today."

We had a routine where if neither of us brought our lunch, then she would choose what we would eat for that day. I had the option of where to go to get it, but whatever she chose was what we ate. After I ran out and picked it up, we would sit in my office and eat together.

Cassandra was the best office manager and assistant that I have had since I started the company and she was worth every penny of her salary. She kept me on my toes and seemed to have the right answer before I could even ask the question.

Our daily lunches together were not only a chance for us to informally talk about the company but they also allowed us to fill each other in on the goings on of our personal lives. Cassandra was more like a baby sister than an employee and I enjoyed our lunches together.

"That's cool. Let me get them for you," she said as she turned to walk out my office.

I was sending one final email, when she walked back in and handed me her keys.

"Same thing as usual?" I asked, taking them from her. Cassandra always wanted the exact same thing every time. She never varied from this, but as was our routine, I always asked.

"You know it," she said as she walked out of my office.

Just as I had gotten in and started the engine in Cassandra's powder blue Toyota Camry, I felt my cell phone vibrating in my pocket. I pulled it out and saw on the display that it was Greg calling. I put in my ear buds and answered the call.

"Whattup, homie?" I said in greeting as I pulled out of the parking lot.

"Can't call it," he answered. "Where you watching the game on Thursday?" he asked, getting right to the point of his phone call.

"Haven't thought about it. Why? What's up?" I asked.

"Nothing really," he said. "I've been doing some thinking and wanted to plan out my week. I decided to call your punk ass and see what you had on tap for Thursday night. Then I was going to figure out the rest of my weekend."

"Punk ass?" I said, feigning displeasure. "Every time I talk to you, I have to ask myself, 'why are we friends?' I haven't even thought about it to be honest. I was going to watch it at home but we can go watch it at Dugan's. What were you thinking about, anyway?"

"Cool. We can do that," he said, completely ignoring my question.

"Sounds like a plan. Just know that you're driving," I replied. "Better yet, I'll drive because I know your behind's going to be sipping on something."

"Damn right," he said, laughing. "I plan on getting my drink on so I'll leave the driving to your non-alcohol, sweet tea drinking ass. Just give me a call before you come through,"

"Whatever, man," I said, laughing at his comment. He always gave me hell about me only drinking tea whenever we went out. It was a rare occasion for me to drink and Greg never missed an opportunity to give me grief about it. "I'll give Walter a call in a few and see if he wants to roll with us."

"Walter? You think he's going to get permission to get out the house?" Greg asked.

"Probably not, but I'll call him and see."

"Okay, cool."

"So, what were you thinking about?" I asked again.

"I'll holla at you later," Greg said and hung up.

I couldn't do anything but laugh as I pulled out my ear buds.

I sat back and turned up the radio and let my mind wander. It would be good to chill with my boys. It had been a while since we all hung out and I needed the distraction. My routine of doing nothing on the weekends and even worse, doing nothing by myself, was really getting old. I had reached a certain level of financial success, but not having anyone to celebrate those successes with was not a good thing. There were only so many toys that I could purchase to serve as distractions. I yearned to have that special someone to share both my successes and my time with.

I glanced over at my cellphone on the passenger seat. Greg wasn't the only one that had been thinking about a few things over the weekend. I thought about the phone call that I started to make the other day but decided against it.

Maybe I need to go ahead and make that call, I thought as I pulled into the China Cafeteria parking lot. I decided to call Walter first to see if he could hang out with us. No matter what, I am going to call her today.

11

Stacey

I was in deep concentration, reviewing several pictures of a gorgeous house in Roswell that a new client was interested in purchasing. The shrill ringing of my office phone cut through my quiet office, startling me in the process.

"Twiggs Reality," I said as I picked up the receiver.

"So how'd it go?" Ethan asked without preamble.

"Hello to you too, Sir," I said. "I don't get a 'Hello' or a 'Good morning?' Just right to it, huh?"

"Good morning, Stacey." Ethan huffed with an annoyed sigh. "So how did it go this weekend?"

"This weekend went wonderfully well, thank you for asking," I replied cheerily. "My Saints won, I went grocery shopping, spent time with Brianna, met a new client, and did laundry. Oh yeah, I got my car washed too. I had a great weekend even though you waited until now to ask me about it. How was your weekend?"

There was silence on the line for a few seconds before he spoke again. "Don't play coy with me, woman. You know exactly what I'm talking about. How'd it go with Walter?"

"Things actually went very well," I said, laughing. "Your friend's a really nice guy. He decided on a nice townhouse in Lithonia and already put in an offer to buy it."

"I bet it did go well," Ethan said in a sarcastic tone.

"Yes, boy! It went well. Nothing more, nothing less," I retorted. "Like I said, we looked at a few houses and he found one that he was interested in. We went through all the details to move forward over lunch."

"So y'all had a date, huh?" Ethan said, totally ignoring everything that I had said, hearing only what he wanted to hear.

"No. We did not have a date," I said. "Let me try this again and I'll talk real slow so you can understand. We. Had. A. Business. Meeting. Over. Lunch. There's a big difference a meeting and a date, Sir," I said, stressing the word 'meeting'. I was doing everything possible to stop him before he could gather any more momentum. I knew him too well and once he got started, there was no stopping him.

"As I stated earlier, we went over the documentation for the house that he wants to purchase," I continued. "I walked him through the process of buying a home so that he would know what to expect moving forward. You know, the exact same thing I did when you were buying your house turned bachelor pad, remember?"

"That's not what he said," Ethan said in a conspiratorial manner, ignoring my question.

My heart skipped a beat when he said that.

"Oh, really?" I was trying my best to sound unfazed by his comment, but knew that I wasn't even coming close to pulling it off.

"And if I recall," he continued, "before I bought my house, we went back to your office and took care of the paperwork. I don't recall any 'business meetings over lunch' when you were working with me."

"Whatever!" I said, "I offered but we worked at my office because your cheap behind didn't want to spend any money on lunch, even when I told you that I would pick up the check."

"Oh, yeah. I forgot about that," he said, laughing. "And I'm frugal, not cheap, thank you. But all that aside, Mr. Olympia told me that he was very impressed with you. In fact, the last time he was that excited was when the double-issue of *Muscle and Fitness* magazine came out."

"Boy, you know you need to stop," I said, laughing. "And I'm sure that he didn't say anything about me. Our meeting was purely professional."

"Mmm hmmm. Sure it was," Ethan said, the sarcasm back in his tone. "I don't know what you two talked about over your 'business meeting over lunch', but it's like y'all are back in high school the way y'all acting. Knowing good and damn well that y'all both digging each other but neither one of y'all wanting to admit it."

Ethan took on a more serious tone and said, "I'll tell you this though, Stacey. You and I have been friends for a long time and you know how much I care about you. Even though me and Walter are cool, I want you to be careful with him. He's in a crazy personal situation he needs to work out. He's my friend also, so I'm kind of in the middle here. I'm not going to tell my boy's business because

I'm not that kind of dude. I wouldn't betray his confidence just like I wouldn't betray yours. Just be careful and make sure you know what you're getting into, okay?"

I took a second to process what he was saying.

"Ethan, I understand where you're coming from," I said soberly. "I wouldn't ask anything like that of you. I respect our friendship too much to put you in that position."

"Don't get me wrong, Stacey," he said, "Walter's a cool guy. A real good guy actually. It bugs the mess out of me when I look at where he is and who he's with. He made the choice but I know that he could do so much better."

"I don't know about all of that," I replied. "He told me that he was in some sort of a relationship but we really didn't have that type of talk yet. I do agree that he's a very interesting guy just from our brief time this past weekend. I'd be lying if I said I wouldn't mind getting to know him better. However, you know better than most that I've been hurt too many times in the past. I don't want to go through that kind of pain again, so for right now, I'm watching my step."

"Cool," Ethan said, the relief evident in his voice. "Him asking about you. You asking about him. And I'm stuck in the middle. I got King Kong asking me about the skinny white chick that he wants to take up to the top of a building. Not a good look at all!"

"Boy, please! I'm far from skinny and even further from being white," I said, laughing and grateful for him lightening the mood. "Ethan, I've got to go. I'll give you a call later on, okay?"

"That's cool. Hit me up," he said and we ended the call.

For a long while, I sat at my desk, looking at the clouds through my office window. I kept replaying the conversation in my mind, Ethan's words of warning playing over and over like a CD set on repeat.

12

Angel

*M*y mind was a million miles away and nowhere close to being focused on the stack of reports piled on my desk beside me. I stood by the large window, sipping on a cup of hot green tea, looking through the clear glass at the traffic streaming by on the highway in the distance. The sky was a hazy blue with an occasional cotton puff of a cloud floating lazily by.

I had just put my cell phone down on one of the many stacks after ending a conversation with my friend. Both my mind and my heart were still racing as I replayed our talk. He had called me on his break, but the conversation took a bad turn when I asked him for what seemed like the millionth time for us to go out on a real date. I loved his company, but I just wanted more.

The discussion ended with him getting frustrated with me and saying that he would call me later. I knew he was getting tired of my constant pleas for us to do more together. He told me that things had been a little slow at the shop the past few weeks but he assured me we would go out soon when things picked up. I told him I understood but truthfully, I was getting tired of us not doing anything beyond staying in at his house or mine and watching movies. As much as I was starting to care for him, it wasn't right that I was having to pay the price for his financial shortcomings. That was not fair to me or to us. We had been going in circles about this for the past few weeks and I was really starting to lose patience with him.

My thoughts were interrupted by the alert on my desk phone telling me I was receiving an inter-office call from one of my coworkers.

"Angel speaking," I answered in a clipped tone so the caller would know that I was not in the mood for chit-chat and get right to the point.

"Hello, Angel," the smooth baritone voice said.

"Hey, Cory. What's up?" I answered, wondering why he was calling me.

Cory Peterson was a senior account manager for the advertising and marketing firm that we both worked for, Port Consultants. We met on a company picnic at Six Flags Over Georgia a few months earlier and he'd been pursuing me ever since. Something about our initial meeting turned me off about him, so I usually found an excuse to turn down his offers for dinners and nights on the town.

He was rumored to be up for a promotion to be the next Vice President of Public Relations once the current VP announced his retirement. I knew that once he got that position along with the six-figure salary that came with it, he would become even more sought after than ever by all the single women in Atlanta.

Cory was tall with the trim, athletic build of a runner. Incredibly sexy with light mocha skin and thick, wavy hair, he was always impeccably dressed in tailored suits. He carried himself with an air of confidence that made him even more attractive. He had been featured in the society pages of the newspaper several times in the last few months. In fact was just listed as one of Atlanta's most eligible bachelors in several of the local social lifestyle magazines.

Here it was that I had this fine, successful, wealthy specimen of a man trying to take me out and giving me the attention that thousands of women would give their left nipple for, and here I was squandering the opportunity.

"I hope I didn't call you at a bad time," he said.

"No, you're okay. I was getting ready for the morning conference call but I have a few minutes," I responded.

"Cool. I'll make it quick then," he said. "You know Maxwell's going to be at the Fox Theater in a few weeks, right?"

"Of course," I said. "The show sold out right after they announced it."

"That's right," he said. "Well, I was able to cop two tickets and I would love for you to go with me to the concert. Maybe grab some dinner too. How does that sound?"

I was silent for a few moments as I mulled over his offer. My girls and I talked about the concert but we didn't even have a chance to get tickets because they sold out so quickly. Seats were so expensive that I had long since written off attending the concert.

"Oh, and did I mention that the tickets were on the front row?" Boasting nonchalantly, his question showcased the sales skills he used when he was trying to close the deal with one of our clients. "Every time I've asked you out before, you always say no for one reason or another. Before you say no this time, how about you take a few days to think about it?"

Maybe his calling to ask me out was a sign, I wondered to myself. I thought about what I wanted and realized that it would be foolish to pass up the chance to go to what I knew would be a great show with a great guy.

"You know what, Cory? I'll be happy to go with you," I said with a smile on my face.

"Really?" he said, not being able to hide his surprise. He obviously was not expecting me to accept his invitation so readily and was caught off guard by my quick response. His persistence paid off in the end and he had finally gotten me to take him up on one of his offers.

"Cool!" he said, recovering quickly and sounding excited. "I actually thought you'd brush me off like you usually do. I knew sooner or later you would give in."

"I guess today's your lucky day," I said, laughing at his comment.

"Yours too," he said confidently. "I'll call you again before the weekend of the show. See you then."

I put my phone back in its cradle and leaned back in my chair. Without a doubt, Cory met my list of requirements for what I wanted in a man. I deserved the best that life had to offer and Cory could definitely give those things to me. *I owed it to myself to give him a chance, right?* But was this really what I wanted? I just wanted to be happy and it seemed that I would never be totally happy with my friend.

Was I being impatient? I didn't think I was but there was a nagging voice inside of me was telling me I was not making the right decision. I stood there staring into space thinking about this for more than thirty minutes. If it wasn't for the alarm buzzing to remind me about the conference call, I might have sat there all day, still dwelling on my situation.

13

Walter

I had just taken my cell phone out of my pocket and placed it on the smooth, stainless steel surface of my desk when it began ringing. The loud ring tone surprised me because I usually kept it on vibrate alert whenever I was in the office.

"Hello." The caller-ID showed Ethan's name and I made the quick decision to take the call. He never called me at work, so I was hoping this had something to do with Stacey.

I lowered the phone, turned to the client in my office, and whispered, "I'll be right back. I have to take this."

I stepped into the hallway and closed my office door behind me. "Ethan, what's up?" I asked into the phone, hoping that he would make it quick so that I could get back to my client.

"Yes, hello," he said, speaking in an exaggerated high-pitched, hillbilly voice complete with the southern twang. "My name's

Jeremiah Jones and I'm looking for a personal trainer. I wanna be so skrong and swole up that I can't scratch my own butt. Can you help me with that, pardner?"

"Ethan, what the hell do you want?" I asked, upset that this idiot was calling me with his foolishness. It was hard to believe that this clown was a successful businessman.

"My bad, big homie," he said, cracking up laughing.

"Yeah, your bad. What do you want?" I hissed. "I've got a new client that I just left alone in my office to take your stupid phone call."

Ethan knew that I was one of the best physical therapists on the staff and as such, I was way too busy to be playing around with him.

"Okay, okay. Calm your nerves," he said. "I was calling your uptight behind to see what you were getting into on Thursday. Me and Greg are going to Dugan's to watch the Falcons/Dolphins game. Can you talk to the warden and see about getting a hall pass to hang out with us?"

"What time?" I asked, distracted by my client who had stuck his head in the hall and was glaring at me.

"How much longer?" he demanded.

"I'm sorry, Mr. Bryant," I said apologetically, bringing the phone down from my ear. "It's my mom."

His features softened and he nodded his head in understanding.

"I'll be right there. Give me two minutes, please," I said.

"Okay. Fine." He huffed before going back into the office and closing the door behind him.

"Yeah, I'll roll with y'all," I said, returning my attention to Ethan.

"That's whassup!" he said. "I can't believe it! You're actually going to hang with the fellas? Are you sure that the witch-I mean the wife or whatever the hell she's supposed to be is going to let you off your leash long enough to go out and play?"

"Whatever, man," I said, wincing from the truth of his comment about Darlene.

"Whatever, hell," he said. "I'll believe it when I see it. Anyway, if you say that you're going, then I'll take your word for it. We'll be at your spot to pick you up around sevenish, so be ready."

"Okay. Seven's cool. I ll be ready," I said.

"Cool," he said. "Please keep in mind that we're going to a sports bar, not a damn Mr. Universe competition so please dress accordingly."

I pinched the bridge of my nose in frustration. This dude knew just how to work my nerves.

"What that means," he continued, "is that you don't need to be wearing that pink speedo with your chest all oiled up like you did last time. All out in public looking like the Grand Marshall at a Pride parade."

I hung up the phone at that. Ethan never missed a chance to get a dig in and I had to grudgingly admit that last one was kind of funny.

I paused before going back into my office to make sure that I turned off the ringer before putting the phone back into my pocket.

After my meeting, I was going over my notes and preparing to enter them into the clinic's client database. As soon as I saw the splash screen for the software, my mind instantly went to Darlene. I flashed back on my earlier conversation with Ethan, and he was right in that ever since I had been with Darlene, it seemed that it took an Act of Congress for me to go out with my friends. I knew that Darlene didn't care for any of them and especially did not like Ethan at all.

Sadly, I felt the same way about her friends. I didn't care for any of them, male or female, that I had met over the time we were together. No matter how hard I tried to get out of going, Darlene would still drag me to all of her social gatherings. I was forced to have to be around what had to be the fakest set of people I had ever come across.

I really could not stand any of them, but I was still pleasant, no matter the occasion. She didn't extend the same courtesy to my friends, however. She was very aloof, bordering on rude, in her interactions with them.

Pushing away from the computer, I looked at the clock hanging on the opposite wall. A few more hours and I would have to go home. I stopped and thought about this. I would rather drag out my time at the office and stay there, finishing paperwork or other mundane tasks than leave. I dreaded going home more and more each day and that depressed me so much. I wanted someone that made it so that when the clock announced at the end of the work day, I would be happy to leave. Instead, there were many days where I would be in my office until well after seven in the evening reading, watching television, anything to delay having to leave.

Home is where the heart is supposed to be. I knew right then and there that I had to get her out of my house. I had to get her out of my life. Period, point blank.

When I told Darlene before that she had to leave, she acted like I was just whistling in the wind and paid me no attention. It was time for me to handle this.

Before I could deal with Darlene, I decided to take a step towards what would hopefully be my future. Moving my mouse to bring up my desktop, I opened the browser and typed in the web address. After looking at the site for a few moments, I found just what I was looking for. Reading from the business card, I filled in the ship-to address, entered my credit card information, and completed the purchase. I then shut down the computer, gathered up my things, and prepared to make the long ride home.

14

Stacey

The phone had been ringing off the hook lately with new clients seeking either to purchase a new home or trying to sell their current one. I was wrapping up yet another call from a new client that had been referred to me.

"No problem, Mrs. Williams. I believe I have everything I need to get started. I'll put together a few homes for you to view and we'll take it from there."

No sooner had I hung up and was making a few notes to myself on the calendar app on my iPad, my cell phone started buzzing with another incoming call.

Checking the caller ID display, I saw that it was Angel.

"Hey, Boo," I said.

"Hey, girl. What's up with you?"

"Not much over here. Just trying to get this week planned out. Looks like it's going to be another busy one. I'm not complaining though."

"I bet you aren't. Looks like I'm going to have a good week too."

"Oh, really? How so? What's going on at work?"

"No, it's not the job," she replied with a cheerful tone. "Well, not exactly. The job's involved but not like that. As far as work's concerned though, things are actually going well for a change. We've been busy as hell trying to finalize a few of our major clients' projects, but beyond that, it's business as usual."

"So what is it then?" I asked, my curiosity rising.

"You remember that guy at my job named Cory?" she said.

"Sure, you mentioned him a few times a while back," I answered, returning my attention back to my iPad. "If I recall, you said he's rich, handsome, and single and has asked you out a few times. He sounds like a great catch but you always turn him down for some unknown reason. What about him?"

"Yes, that's him," she said. "And yes, I did always turn him down. Well, things have changed. He just called me up and asked me out, but this time I said yes! And Guess what? You won't believe this!"

"Oh really now? What is it?" I asked, stopping working to focus on what she was saying.

"We're going to the Maxwell concert! And front row seats no less!" she shrieked.

"Say what?" I asked incredulously. "I thought it was sold out? How did he get tickets? And then front row seats?"

"He didn't say and I didn't ask," she said. "I'll be honest. I almost said no again but something told me to take the plunge. Like I told you the other day, I decided that it was time for me to take care of me. My friend is who I'd love to be with but I can't wait any longer."

I reclined in my chair and listened quietly as Angel opened up and let all of the confusion and frustration pour out. Even though it was a busy morning we still made time to listen to each other.

"I know Cory's the kind of man that I think I need to be with," she continued. "He has the money, the career, the car, the connections, everything. But…well, I don't know what it is. It's just that I'm really starting to care more about my friend, but I don't know where that would really go. Cory's a damn good catch and is right there waiting. It's time for me to make that move and the first step is us going out to the concert."

"Well, that's a lot for you to consider," I said finally. "I'll tell you that I really don't know what to say about your 'friend', as you like to call him. I don't know anything about him except for the occasional mention of him here and there. You're right. You and your friend are not in an exclusive relationship. I think that you should give Cory a chance because he sounds like the kind of man that you have wanted for as long as I can remember. From all that you've told me about him, he seems to have everything that you're looking for. But the fact that you can't at the very least tell me his name instead of calling him 'my friend' also speaks volumes."

"I can understand that," she said. "It's really because I didn't want to say too much about him just yet. I'm just so frustrated with the whole situation."

"I'm sure you're frustrated," I said. "I'd be too if I were in your position. I guess the only thing I can say is if your friend is truly just a friend, then he won't mind you going out with another friend, right? If he's more or at least wants to be more, then he needs to step his game up. You're worth it, girl."

"Yeah, I know," she said, but without any confidence in her voice.

"But I do know this much though, I'm going to be at that concert," she said with a laugh. "I'm going to go and watch that sexy ass Maxwell sing and have some fun for a change."

"I'm so jealous of you right now," I said, joining in with her laughter. "You know what? Get off my phone! I can't even talk to you anymore."

"Whatever! Don't hate! I'll call you later," she said and hung up.

I took a few minutes and thought about Angel's relationship dilemma. I knew that she was seeking the same thing that we all wanted, which was a real love from someone that we could call our own. I thought about my own love pursuits and how they always seemed to end in futility.

Even though her criteria for the perfect man seemed to be rooted more in what was in his wallet as opposed to what was in his heart, she just wanted to find happiness. I wanted the same and didn't think that was asking for too much.

15

Ethan

As much as I tried, I could not concentrate on any of the items on the long list of things that I had to do today. For the last thirty minutes, I had been sitting in my office with the door closed, staring off into space, my mind wandering everywhere, focusing on nothing.

I finally gave up trying to get any work done and pulled up the Pandora website on my computer. Kicking my feet up on my desk, I began listening to my Jaheim station and relaxed to the random R&B selections playing through the surround sound speakers positioned on the walls around my office.

I closed my eyes and listened as Anthony Hamilton passionately crooned his song, his emotion-filled words pouring out as he tried to explain to his special lady that the point of it all, the reason of it all, was that he loved her.

Is that really all there is to it? I asked myself as I absorbed the powerful lyrics and stared at the photos that hung on my office wall.

As the song came to an end, I took my feet down from my desk where they had been comfortably propped and muted the volume.

It was early Wednesday afternoon and Cassandra and I had just finished eating lunch together. Her choice for today was Mexican food, so we ate taco salads along with chips and salsa from our favorite Mexican spot.

She had been in the middle of telling me about her and Jerome, but I was unable to concentrate on anything that she was saying. My mind was instead focused on the dilemma that I had been wrestling with for far too long. It was not in my nature to procrastinate, so as soon as we finished eating and she left my office, I made up my mind to make the call. That turned out to be harder to do than I could imagine. I took a deep breath before I reached over and grabbed my cell phone from my desk.

I pushed SEND on the entry for 'Monica Nolastname' and listened as the phone rang in my ear.

What was I doing? I thought, my will faltering as questions and doubt began flooding my mind. *What was the point? Would she remember me? If I were her, would I remember someone that I had met over six months ago? Why even bother with someone who lives all the way in New Orleans?*

I thought about that last question. It's not that I didn't mind travelling; hell, I loved it. Not only was I currently working towards getting my pilot's license, I used to drive trucks all across the country. I gave up driving and got off the road in order to build my business.

I knew from painful experience the difficulties of long-distance relationships.

Trying to start something with a person who lives in the same area code as you is hard enough, but when you have someone that lives hundreds of miles away, things are that much harder. Those lonely nights knowing that your love is nowhere close to you become more and more difficult to bear, no matter how good everything else might be.

"Sweet Sinsations, Bernard speaking. How may I help you?" an enthusiastic male voice said, interrupting my thoughts and bringing me back to reality.

"Yes, thank you," I said, clearing my throat nervously. "May I speak with Monica, please?"

"I'm sorry, sir. Monica's out of the store. She's at our new Atlanta store and will be there all month. Is there anything that I could help you with?"

"Atlanta? You guys have a store here?" I asked in disbelief. I almost dropped the phone at hearing this. *An Atlanta store? Monica is here in Atlanta?*

"Yes, sir! We sure do. We just opened it a few months ago and it's doing great. Much better than we could've hoped."

The pride in Bernard's voice brought a smile to my face.

"Congratulations!" I said. "Are you her husband?"

I closed my eyes and crossed my fingers while I waited on his answer.

"Uhhm, no. Monica's my mom. Eww!" he said with a laugh. "I'm running the New Orleans store while she's in Atlanta."

"Oh, she's your mom," I said, breathing a sigh of relief.

"Yes, she's my mom. And I noticed you used the word 'here' so I'm guessing that you're in Atlanta?"

"Very perceptive," I said. "Yes, I'm on the east side of town. The Stone Mountain area. I met Monica a while back and was calling to check on her. Hearing that you guys have opened a second location, I'm guessing that things are going very well."

"Yes, things are picking up," he said proudly. "You should give Mom, I mean Monica, a call. Better yet, go visit the store and buy a few cupcakes while you're there," he said with a laugh.

"I might just do that," I said, sitting down behind my desk. I grabbed a pen and reached for a Post-it note. "What's the number for the store?"

He recited the number and gave me the address as well.

"Thank you," I said, jotting down the information and ending the call.

This was truly unexpected, I thought as I reclined in my chair. I laced my fingers together behind my head and stared up at the ceiling, pondering my next move.

I thought about things for a few minutes and slowly a plan began to develop. Picking up the phone, I stood and paced as I dialed the number that Bernard had just given me.

"Sweet Sinsations, Monica speaking," she said in that sultry voice that I remembered so well.

There was a brief silence as she waited for me to speak and as I tried to find words to say.

"Hello? May I help you?" she asked again.

"Um...yes. Hel...hello," I finally said, my usual confidence was gone, replaced by nervous excitement. "I'd like to order something for a friend of mine but I'm not sure what to get. Could you help me with that, please?"

"Certainly! I'd be happy to help," she said brightly.

"We have a large selection of cupcakes, brownies, and other baked items. I'm sure we can find something that your friend would enjoy. Is your friend a male or female?"

"Female," I answered, sitting back down behind my desk and feeling myself becoming more relaxed as we spoke.

"Cool beans," Monica said. "Could you tell me what her tastes are? What kinds of cake does she like? What type of alcohol does she like? The more information you can give me, the more options I'll be able to present to you."

"To be honest, I really don't know. I just met her and really haven't learned that much about her. Yet. How about this? What's your favorite item?"

I crossed my fingers and hoped she would answer without becoming too suspicious or recognize my voice. I doubted that she would after all the time that had passed, but I did not want to risk it.

"Well, my personal favorite is our French Connection Cupcake. It's a delicious, moist white cake infused with Grand Marnier liqueur and top shelf cognac. I absolutely love it and I'm sure your friend will too."

"Wow, that sounds pretty good," I said. I wasn't a big cake person, but hearing that description had my mouth watering for some all of a sudden. "That's a lot of liquor! I'm getting a buzz just thinking about it. I'll take a dozen."

"Great! Thank you," she said, and I could tell she was genuinely happy to have a new customer.

"When would you like to pick them up?" she asked.

"Let's see," I said as I glanced at my watch. "How about today? Around five, maybe? Will that be enough time?"

"Yes, that should be fine. I'll have them ready and waiting for you at five this afternoon."

She gave me the final price along with the address of her store and we ended the call.

As I stared at the clock hanging on my wall, I knew that in a few more hours, I would know if I had made the right decision to call her.

16

Angel

It seemed the minute I came back from lunch and sat down, my cell phone began to ring. Hoping it was my cable company following up on my complaint call from earlier this morning, I picked it up and saw from the caller-ID display that it was my friend instead.

"Hey, there!" I said, not being able to hide the surprise in my voice. I wasn't expecting to hear from him this early in the day. He usually called me around five or six in the evening when he knew I would be leaving the office and headed home. The last time he called me this early, we ended up in an argument so I hoped this conversation didn't end up the same way.

"What's going on?" I asked, "You took the day off? Trying to get some rest?"

"Whatever," he said, laughing. "You're the one that needs to be soaking in Epsom salts to get your legs back under control. I saw you doing the 'stanky leg' dance when you got out the bed and tried to walk to the bathroom."

I burst out laughing because it was so true. After our last time together, I was walking like a drunken runway model in six inch stiletto heels.

"On the real though, you did cross my mind," he said, "I was taking a customer's car for a test drive and heard a commercial on the radio. It made me think about you so I decided to call."

"Oh really?" I asked, chuckling. "Thinking about me or just certain parts of me?"

"Well, come to think about it," he said, laughing, "It was a commercial for a restaurant, so yeah I did think about eating. I'm glad this guy had some napkins in his car because my mouth started watering."

"Wow!" I exclaimed, my mind filling with the image of him working his oral magic. Once again, I felt the return of that familiar warmth that seemed to occur whenever we got together.

"So is that why you called me?" I said, trying to refocus. "You just wanted to tell me you were thinking about me and all my beautiful body parts?"

"Nah, sexy. That's not why at all," he replied. "I was actually calling to see what you were doing this weekend. I know we got into it the other day about us never going anywhere or doing anything outside of the bedroom. Well, I've been thinking about what you said and I want to take you out. On a real date. You know, dinner, the movies, all that. What do you think?"

I couldn't believe it. After months of me wondering if he was ever going to take me out, he finally decided to come through.

Maybe I should go and buy a lottery ticket, I thought as I reflected on my change of romantic fortune. I had to be on some sort of lucky streak because things were going fabulously well for me lately. First Cory asks me out a few days earlier and now, out of the blue my friend calls wanting to take me out as well.

This just seemed to be par for the course as far as my love life was concerned. It was either feast or famine. For months at a time, I would go without as much as a phone call from a guy, much less having one ask me out on a date. On more occasions than I cared to count, I wasn't cuddled up in a man's arms. Instead I would spend lonely weekends curled up with my latest Netflix selection. But as fate would have it, here I was with both my friend and Cory wanting to take me out on back-to-back weekends.

"Really?" I asked, hardly able to contain my excitement. "Where are we going? What did you have in mind?"

"Well, I figured we could keep it simple. Nothing like dinner and a movie, right?" he said enthusiastically, his voice full of pride. "We could go to the movies but only after we go and get some seafood. Your favorite, right?"

"Really?" I asked, squealing in delight. *Could this get any better?* I thought. Not only was I happy that he said seafood, which was in fact my absolute favorite, I really loved the fact that he knew enough about me to know what my likes were.

"Yes, seafood," he said, laughing at my outburst. "We're going to go to dinner at Red Lobster and then go check out that new Denzel joint. The previews looked pretty good and I've wanted to check it out for a while."

"Red Lobster?" I said, all of the excitement draining out of me in that instant. Really? Red Lobster? I appreciated the gesture more than anything, but I really hoped for something more upscale than Red Lobster on our first official date.

"Yeah, Red Lobster," he said, the confusion evident in his tone. "I thought you liked seafood? Is there something wrong?"

"No, nothing's wrong," I said, doing what I usually did and not really telling him exactly what I wanted. Stacey's words came rushing back to me as I remembered her telling me that if I wanted something from a man, then the only way he would know is for me to tell him. I took a few moments to try and find the right words to express to him exactly what I wanted.

"The movie is fine, baby," I began. "But can we go to Pappadeaux instead of Red Lobster?"

I absolutely loved Pappadeaux. Even though their prices were considerably higher than Red Lobster's, I believe that I was worth it and much more.

"Wow." he said in a quiet exhale. "I really wasn't expecting that. Wasn't expecting that at all."

"What weren't you expecting?" I asked. I know that he wasn't trying to catch an attitude because I wanted something better than Red Lobster. "I do want us to go out. Lord knows I've been asking you to take me somewhere. I just want it to be somewhere nice. Somewhere classy. Is that asking for too much? If it is, please let me know."

There was a brief silence on the phone before he spoke.

"Nah, Angel," he said with resignation. "Pappadeaux is fine. I'll work it out."

"Great!" I said, ignoring his pouting as my excitement returned. "So what time are you coming to get me?"

"I'll pick you up at seven on Saturday. Is that cool?" he asked.

"Yes. I'll be ready," I said.

"Okay. I'll talk to you later," he said with another deep sigh and hung up without waiting for me to respond.

I didn't know what his problem was but he needed to get over it real quick. I was going to start asking, no, demanding that I get treated to the finer things. If he wanted more out of our relationship, then he needed to bring his 'A' game. Asking to be taken to a nice restaurant was nothing. If he couldn't do that, then as much as I hated to do it, I would have to move on to bigger and better things. There was someone potentially waiting in the wings and if he didn't play his cards right, he would soon find himself replaced.

I sat there for a long while, still holding my phone, looking out my window and smiling in anticipation of the next few weekends.

17

Stacey

I stared in amazement at the beautiful, long-stemmed rainbow roses that were arranged in an adorable, frosted crystal vase. I couldn't hold back my smile as I admired the flowers, wondering just who could have sent them to me.

I had just gotten back from picking up lunch and was enjoying my chicken sandwich when the UPS delivery truck pulled up. I didn't pay much attention to what was being brought in until the driver put the flowers on my desk in front of me.

"Sign here, please," he said, holding out his handheld computer and stylus for me to sign. His words brought me back to reality and I scrawled my name across the electronic screen.

"What's the last name?" he asked as he turned to head out the door, his thumbs positioned over the small keypad, ready to enter the information.

"Twiggs," I answered distractedly, my attention transfixed on the flowers.

I gently rubbed one of the soft petals between my fingers as I read the attached card:

Stacey,

Thank you for showing me my future.

-Walter

I pulled out one of the roses and took a deep inhale of the fragrant, delicate flower.

I can't believe he sent these, I thought as I read and reread the simple but thoughtful note.

This was truly unexpected. I knew we had made some sort of connection the other day. I enjoyed the time with him a lot more than I cared to admit and wanted to spend more with him.

After wrapping up our business, we finished eating, however neither one of us wanted to leave. The conversation flowed and we talked about so many different things. Not only was he a physically attractive man, he had a warm and engaging personality as well.

Ever since, I have wanted to give Walter a call. I smiled because him sending me flowers let me know that I was on his mind as well. He had made his move, so maybe I should take the risk and make mine.

I nibbled on some French fries as I slid over to the file cabinet on the side of my desk. Flipping through the tabs, I stopped at the file that was marked with his name. I looked inside and got his cell phone number off the client contact sheet.

Taking a deep breath, I thought about what I would say when I called him. After going back and forth with myself, I decided that instead of calling, I would send him a simple text. I typed a short message:

> *Thank you so much for the flowers. You're more than*
> *welcome. I look forward to being there the rest of the way.*
> *-Stacey*

I looked at my text, reading the words on the screen over and over before finally closing my eyes and hitting SEND. Based on his response when he got the message, I would know how to move forward.

I crossed my fingers as I waited for his return text. After a few minutes without a reply, I wondered if he even got the message. *Did I send it to the right person? Did he look at the message and just laugh? Did I just play myself?*

I went back to eating my lunch, rereading the card for the twentieth time, wondering if I had completely misunderstood the message he was sending. Did I misconstrue his simple gesture of kindness and read more into it than he actually intended? Did my mind blow it out of proportion? Did my heart want it to be a romantic signal from him? I was startled by my cell phone which started ringing on my desk.

Picking it up, I looked at the caller ID. It's him! At most, I thought he would send me a return text, so I definitely was not expecting him to call, especially not so soon.

"Hello," I said hesitantly as I answered the phone.

"Good afternoon," he said in that sexy voice of his.

"I guess you got my text, huh?" I said, giggling like a school girl.

"Yes, I did," he said. "I started to text you back, but I didn't know what to say. When I did think of a response, I'd start typing only to delete it and start over. I finally decided to just call instead. Is that okay?"

"Of course," I said. I was blushing uncontrollably at his comment. "So what was it that you wanted to say that you couldn't put into a text?"

"I forgot now," he said with a hearty laugh. "I'm a little nervous over here, so bear with me."

"You? Nervous?" I said, joining in with his laughter. "I'm over here shaking like I've never talked to a man before. This is so weird."

"Good, I thought it was just me," he said. "I'm glad that you liked the flowers though."

"I love them," I said, "Thank you so much."

"Cool. It's the least I could do," he said, "After our conversation in the restaurant, I was worried that you'd think they were too much. I'm still working on my current situation and I didn't want to do anything until that's over. I did want to do something to express my appreciation of you though."

"Of me?" I asked quietly. I was caught off guard with that.

"Yes," he said softly. "You've been on my mind ever since we met. There's something really special about you. You know that, right?"

"Thank you," was the only response I could give him.

There was a brief lull as if we were both trying to figure out what to do next.

"Hold on for a second," he said. I could hear him talking to someone in the background for a few moments and then he came back on the phone.

"Hey, Stacey," he said, returning to the phone. "I have to go to a meeting. Do you mind if I call you later when I get off?"

I thought about this for a quick beat before answering, "Sure, that's fine."

"Great!" he said happily. "I'll call you around five-thirty this evening."

"Okay, talk to you then," I said as we ended the call.

Lord, help me, I thought as I put my cell phone back on my desk.

I knew that Walter still had someone in his life, and until that was over, there could be nothing between us. No matter how attractive he was, I had to make sure that I kept things at a certain level. The problem was the more I thought about him, the more I talked to him, the more difficult it was for me to try and keep my distance from him. Being really honest with myself, I didn't want to stay away from him.

18

Walter

I took a bite of the Reuben sandwich that the server brought out to me. I closed my eyes and savored the delightfully briny flavor of the corned beef.

My week seemed to be flying by. It was hard to believe that it was already Thursday and the weekend was right around the corner.

I was on my lunch break, gazing out the window beside my booth at Jason's Deli, enjoying this time alone. This had become a part of my daily afternoon routine and was my way of relaxing during my hectic workday.

I preferred taking a later break to avoid the crazy lunch rush crowds. When everyone in the surrounding area was back at work in their offices after normal lunch hours, I would then take my break. There were no long lines to fight through and I had my choice of places to sit as I enjoyed my time.

As I ate, I thought about the previous weekend and the events that happened earlier this week.

I was under the impression that I had broken up with Darlene in no uncertain terms, but instead she seemed to be even more involved than ever before. To her, it was like our conversation at the mall hadn't even occurred. Darlene was going along like it was business as usual and my words and feelings did not matter.

When we left the mall last weekend, she was quiet for the entire ride home. She silently looked out of the window with an expressionless stare.

The minute we arrived to the apartment, she had gotten out of the car and shut her door. She then marched inside with her normal confident stride and went straight into the bedroom, put on a pair of black leggings, T-shirt, before into the kitchen.

I didn't know what was going on with her strange behavior but I couldn't do anything but play along. I was helpless for the time being until I moved into my new home.

I went to the living room and turned on the television and tried to watch the end of the late game. This was impossible, however, because my mind was in a daze and I couldn't seem to concentrate on anything.

An hour or so had past without me even realizing as I sat there mulling over my situation. I was completely unaware of anything that was going on around me.

I was jolted back to reality by the plate of food along with the tall glass of freshly brewed iced tea that Darlene put in front of me. I was really thrown for a loop as I took in the sight and smell of the delicious pan-roasted chicken thighs, spinach, white rice, and sweet cornbread.

I sat there, looking at the plate of food, trying to figure out what Darlene was trying to do. She rarely if ever cooked anything, much less one of my favorite meals.

"Wow," I said in disbelief. "This looks great. What's the occasion?"

"There's nothing special, baby. Does there need to be a reason for me to want to take care of my man?" she responded sweetly. "I know you love when I cook this for you, right? Well, I haven't made them in a while. You just go ahead and eat, okay. When you're finished, come to the bedroom. I'll have another surprise waiting for you in there too."

She said this last comment with a suggestive smile on her face. She then turned and walked down the hallway to the bedroom.

If I wasn't already in an absolute state of confusion this really pushed me over the edge.

"Darlene," I said cautiously. "I'm not sure what's going on but I don't think that's a good idea. In fact, I know it wouldn't be a good idea at all. As much as I appreciate you cooking for me, I really don't think we need to do that."

"And why not?" she asked, stopping to turn and look at me with a look of mild amusement on her face.

"I just don't, Darlene," I said, looking directly into her eyes, trying my best to understand what was going through her mind. Did she not hear anything I said to her earlier? Did she think I didn't mean what I said?

"I think you're worrying too much, Walter. Now please eat your dinner and then meet me in the bedroom," she said with finality and then turned and went into the room, closing the door behind her.

This is nuts!

As much as I didn't want to eat for fear of something crazy like the food being poisoned, the delicious aroma coming from the plate in front of me was absolutely intoxicating. I reluctantly took a forkful of spinach and rice into my mouth. It was outstanding! I quickly shoveled in another mouthful, not realizing just how hungry I was. After several more huge forkfuls, the plate was almost halfway finished before I knew it.

I paused long enough to take a sip of the iced tea and smiled with pleasure. She had sweetened the brew just the way I liked it. I proceeded to dig into the rest of the meal and before long, I had nothing but a plate of bones in front of me.

A good ten minutes had passed since I had finished eating, and with each tick of the clock, I looked uneasily at the bedroom door. I dreaded going in there, but I knew that I had to, even if it was to just brush my teeth, since I had to pass through there in order to get to the bathroom.

Finally, I gathered my courage and got to my feet. This had to be done and I couldn't put it off any longer. I picked up my dishes and took them into the kitchen, ran some water on them to rinse them off before putting them in the sink. I was acutely aware of the fact that I was using the mundane chore to stall for time.

Let's get this over with, I thought as I headed into the bedroom.

As I entered, the first thing that struck me was that the overhead lights were off. The only light came from several candles that were placed around the room. They cast a soft glow, barely illuminating Darlene's body as she lay in the bed.

The mellow sounds of the Isley Brothers singing "Between the Sheets" filled the room. The music started playing as soon as I opened the door, indicating that Darlene had been waiting on me and had hit the play key with the radio's remote control.

I walked in the room cautiously, closing the door behind me, not sure what my next move was going to be. Should I turn on the lights? Should I turn off the music? I was at a total loss because once again, Darlene had taken control of the situation.

"Darlene?" I called, not sure what to expect.

"Yes, my love?" she answered in the most seductive voice I had ever heard from her lips.

Her sexy response sent a shiver up my spine. I was trying to be strong and hold my own, but I felt myself starting to go weak and fall under her spell.

She sat up in the bed, pulling the sheet over her obviously bare breasts.

"Come over here and sit down," she said, gently patting the bed next to her.

The alluring smell of her perfume filled my nostrils as I looked at her body framed in the candlelight. I could not stop the stirring in my boxers. I knew this woman was not who I wanted to be with but I could not fight the urge that was building within me.

I tentatively walked over to the bed and sat down, my back to her, and tried to gather what little resolve I had left. I knew that if I didn't fight back these feelings now, I would never be able to hold back.

"Darlene, I think tha–" I began, but was cut off in mid-sentence as she came up behind me and put her naked body against my back.

I could feel her firm breasts pressed against me and all of the fight instantly drained out of me.

She moved around until she was sitting next to me. I gazed into her eyes, trying to read what she was thinking. Even though I knew I did not love her and at times didn't even like her, right about now I knew exactly what I wanted from her.

Moving even closer to me, she forcefully pressed her lips against mine, initiating a powerful kiss that caused the energy that I was trying to control to explode from within me.

We kissed for what seemed like hours until I finally broke away from her. I couldn't resist it any longer. I moved her back so that I could stand and take off my shirt.

As I stood in front of her, she rubbed her hand against my engorged manhood. The fabric of my gym shorts was straining to contain me and her touch caused me to shiver with pleasure.

Standing there shirtless, looking down at Darlene, I watched as she pulled the drawstring of my shorts, causing them to loosen and fall off my hips, freeing my shaft from its cotton cage.

I couldn't believe this. In all of the years that I had been with Darlene, I could count on one hand the times that she had done what I thought, hoped, prayed that she was going to do.

And she did. As she took me into her warm mouth, my eyes rolled into the back of my head as pleasure overtook me. I was in heaven as she orally embraced my erection, feverishly working her head back and forth so that she could take it all in.

As she worked her magic on me, my knees grew weak, almost buckling several times as I stood there. I had to reach out and grab the headboard in order to keep my balance.

Just as I felt myself reaching that thrilling peak, she abruptly stopped and looked up at me with her most seductive smile.

Her stopping took me off guard and I had to take a few seconds to gather my wits and to allow my eyes to refocus.

Darlene lay on her stomach, splayed across the bed looking up at me, feasting on the look of pleasure that was still pasted on my face. She smiled as she slowly licked her lips, seemingly enjoying the taste that was still on them.

She then very sexily, very slowly, rolled onto her back. With feline agility, Darlene slithered backwards on the bed. She stopped before arching her back, raising her backside up seductively. She lay there, her moist center presented to me, inviting me to partake in the pleasure that lay there.

I took in the scene of her erotic beauty on display in front of me and felt the ache of lust pulling at me. I gazed at her for a few more seconds before I gave in to the urge and moved forward towards her.

In a rush of pent up energy fueled by my frustration with Darlene's antics, I quickly moved onto the bed, and in an instant, I was hovering over her naked form.

I could not wait any longer. I positioned myself between the margins of her moistness before plunging deep into her.

She released a moan of pleasure that echoed throughout the room. As she caught her breath, she opened her eyes and looked at me. It was a look that was so filled with pain that it caused me to pause and consider just what we were doing.

Her eyes told me a completely different story than what her body was saying. Her body was singing the song of pleasure that it was receiving, the beat set by the sound of the headboard rhythmically hitting the wall; however, her eyes were filled with a pain that no amount of sex would be able to erase.

I couldn't continue. I slowly pulled out of her and rolled onto my back, staring blankly at the ceiling as I realized what was happening.

No matter how many meals she cooked, no matter how good the lovemaking was, no matter what she said or did, we would never work. I did not love Darlene and never would.

I had to end this. I had to bring this relationship to a close. I had to do it now.

Darlene rolled on her side and looked at me, her sad eyes filled with fear.

"Did I do something wrong?" she asked softly, pulling the covers over her naked body. "I can do better, baby. Just tell me what you want me to do and I'll do it."

I looked at her and felt a mixture of disgust, compassion, and curiosity. She was revealing a side of her that I had never seen before and I really didn't know how to react.

The sound of a car horn blowing brought me back to the present. I looked and saw that two cars had collided with each other at the intersection across the street. One of the drivers was blowing his horn angrily at the driver of the other car for causing the fender-bender.

Shaking my head, I began to gather my things to leave. I felt that my relationship with Darlene was like those cars—we had come crashing to an end as well.

19

Ethan

A quick glance at the clock on the radio of my GMC Sierra Denali confirmed that I was right on schedule. I was heading to Monica's store to pick up my order and hopefully a little more.

I exited off I-285 and was riding down Glenwood Road, my old stomping grounds where I got into all kinds of dirt as a teenager. Now as I slowly drove along, observing all the closed businesses and blatant poverty, I was saddened at how much things had changed.

After a few minutes, I came to the stop at the traffic light at Line Street and Glenwood. I knew that Candler Road was the next intersection even without the friendly voice of the truck's navigation system alerting me. I had a good idea as to where I was going, but I still entered the address in the GPS anyway just to be safe. I was really beginning to regret this decision as the system annoyingly informed me of each turn every five seconds.

I felt my heart rate increase because I knew that I was only a few minutes away from Monica's store. *What would happen when she saw me? What would she say? What would she do?* All of these thoughts flooded my mind as I waited for the light to turn green.

The light changed and I made the right turn onto Candler. Moments later, the navigation system informed me that my destination was on my left. I realized that Monica's store was right on the corner of Candler and Memorial in what used to be a Subway restaurant.

I pulled into the lot and parked in the space next to a burnt orange, convertible Chevy Camaro SS. Getting out of my truck, I looked around at the area outside of the shop which sat on the intersection of the two busy streets. I was impressed at how good the location was as I observed the traffic passing by the store slowly getting heavier as everyone was getting off work.

I checked my watch and saw that I had timed things perfectly. I knew from visiting her website that the store closed at six today. I wanted to walk in the door right before she closed, and it was a few minutes till closing.

I walked in the shop and saw Monica standing behind the counter with her back facing the door. She was wearing an orange tee shirt tucked into a pair of stretch jeans which she was filling out quite nicely. I took a moment to check out her assets and was very pleased with everything that I saw.

"Hello. I'll be right there with you," she said over her shoulder.

"No problem," I replied, picking up one of the brochure menus that was laying on the counter display.

"Sorry about that, sir. How may I hel-" she began, pausing mid-sentence as soon as she recognized me.

"Ethan Lucas," she said, a sexy smile creasing her face.

It took every bit of self-control that I could muster not to break out into a Holy Ghost praise dance complete with speaking in tongues at the fact that she not only remembered me but remembered my name as well.

"Monica NoLastName. How have you been?" I asked, extending my hand.

"NoLastName?" she said, looking at me curiously as she took my hand in hers.

"Yes. Like Prince or Tamia, right? You never did give me your last name when we met in Seattle. I had your card but it only had your first name and the information for your store in New Orleans. I called there looking for you and that's how I found out that you'd opened this store."

"Oh, yes. That's right. That was a crazy time in my life. I was in the process of closing a few doors and trying to open some new ones. I was a little distracted back then. I'm glad you used the card and called though. Finally."

"I think you being distracted is an understatement. If I recall correctly, your phone was ringing off the hook. And, yes, I'm glad I made the call as well."

There was a brief pause in the conversation and we realized at the same time that we were still holding each other's hand. We smiled at each other before reluctantly releasing hands.

"Langston," she said.

"Hughes? University?" I asked in confusion.

"My last name, silly." She giggled. "My last name is Langston."

"Oh. I didn't know what you were talking about," I said, chuckling.

"Have a seat," she said, motioning to one of the stools by the display counter.

"So what brings you to my store?" she asked, resuming the task that she was working on when I walked in the store.

"Well, I wanted to see you. And I had an order to pick up."

"An order?" she asked, looking up from the box that she was filling with cupcakes.

"Yes, I placed an order earlier today. The French Connection Cupcakes. I ordered a dozen of them and you said I could pick them up this evening. Well, I'm here but what I don't see are my cupcakes," I said, exaggeratedly turning my head left and right as if trying to find something.

"Oh, that was your order? Well, you must not be looking very hard then. Stevie Wonder could see that your cupcakes are right here," she said, laughing and holding up a bright orange box.

"They've been ready and waiting. I think you'll enjoy them. They're my personal favorite."

"Yeah, that's what you said on the phone. That's why I ordered them. In fact, I was hoping we could even enjoy them together."

Her eyebrows shot up with surprise at my statement. I could see her mind working as she thought over my proposal.

Damn, she mouthed silently and took a step back so that she was leaning against the counter behind her. She folded her arms across her chest and stared at me intently for a few moments.

I sat motionless on the stool and waited nervously for her response.

I didn't know how this was going to play out, but I knew that I really wanted to get to know more about this woman.

"You're still bold, I see," she said.

I was beyond relieved that her response was not a flat out 'NO'. I was incredibly excited because this meant that I had a shot if I played my cards right.

"Well...How about we save the cupcakes for dessert?" I asked, trying to contain the nervous excitement bubbling inside me. "I was thinking that we could go grab something to eat. Maybe talk a little bit and then enjoy the cupcakes. How does that sound?"

She looked beyond me to the traffic passing by on the busy street as she mulled over my suggestion.

"When? Where?" she asked, the question directed at me, her gaze still focused on the traffic outside.

"No time like the present. There's a great sushi spot not too far from here. That's if you like sushi. If not, we can go somewhere else."

She looked at me with the brief flicker of a mischievous smile crossing her face as she thought about this.

"Okay. I'm hungry and I love sushi. You know what? I'll take you up on your offer. But don't think that you're gonna get some just because you bought me dinner."

"Whatever!" I said, laughing with relief. "Look here, woman. If I spend my hard-earned money on you, taking you out to fancy meals and what-not, you better put out."

"Well, since you put it that way, Mr. Man, I guess I could give you a lil somethin'-somethin'. But you better super-size my meal dammit!"

There was such ease with which we could talk to each other going all the way to when we first met in Seattle. I was filled with a really good feeling inside.

"Here you go. Since you're buying dinner, I'll take care of dessert. These are on the house," she said, handing me the box. "Wait for me outside while I lock up and finish a few things in the back. I should only be about twenty minutes. Hopefully we won't be gone too long so I'll finish these orders when I get back."

"Cool. Thanks," I said, taking the box from her and following her to the front door.

"I won't be long," she said as she ducked inside and locked the door behind her.

I put the box of cupcakes on the back seat and waited for her to come back out. My palms were sweaty because of how nervous I was. I knew the feeling I had about her was correct just from our few brief conversations. Not only was she beautiful and intelligent, she also had a great sense of humor. I was looking forward to getting to know her even better.

A few minutes passed before Monica reappeared. As she was locking the front door, I got out of the truck and held the passenger door open for her. I was glad I drove my truck today because there was no way I could have pulled this off on my bike.

"Umm...what do I look like just getting into a total stranger's car? You might kidnap me or something," she said, stopping a few feet away from the truck.

"Whatever," I said with a laugh. "The last person that tried to kidnap you probably drove around the block and dropped your ass off right back where they picked you up. They got tired of hearing your yap and said the hell with it. But seriously, I feel where you're coming from. I honestly didn't even think about that. If you want to take your own whip, I completely understand. I'll lead the way and you can just follow me there."

She studied me for a long moment and I could tell she was thinking through the whole situation. Finally, she nodded her head in silent approval, as if having arrived at the right conclusion.

"No, I'll ride with you. I trust you," she said, walking over to the opened door of the truck.

"Thank you," she said, smiling with approval as she climbed in. "I was able to finish that last order, so I don't have to work late tonight."

"That's good to hear," I said, as I started the engine.

"So where are we off to?" she asked

"Sushi Avenue. Have you ever been there?"

"No, I haven't. But I'll take your word that it will be good. If it's not though, be advised that there will be hell to pay."

She looked at me with what was supposed to be a menacing look but the smile on her face let me know that she wasn't serious.

"Oh hell, I hope for my sake that it's good then," I said as I pulled out of the parking lot and headed towards downtown Decatur. On the quick ten minute ride there, Monica and I engaged in small talk about her business and how things had been progressing since she opened her second store a few months ago.

We soon pulled into the Decatur Square, an area of eclectic shops and restaurants right in the heart of the city. I couldn't believe our fortune when we found a good parking space without having to circle the block several times. This meant that it would only be a short walk to the restaurant.

The next two hours were the most refreshing that I have ever spent with a woman. We talked about everything. Usually I had to dumb myself down in order to have a conversation with most of the women that I meet. With her, it was just the opposite. She actually made me have to think, and that kept me actively engaged the whole evening.

We didn't go too deep into personal topics but I never felt like she was hiding anything from me. The vibe I got was that it was more of a cautious approach to me than anything, and I was okay with that. There weren't any awkward silences or pauses as we searched for things to talk about.

After dinner, we drove back to her store, riding in a comfortable silence. We were in our own worlds, wrapped up in our own thoughts. Throughout the trip, I had a sense of comfortable familiarity with her that did not make the quiet trip feel tense in any way.

When we got back, I walked her to her car.

"Well, Mr. Lucas, I can honestly say that I had a great evening. I hope that maybe we can do this again soon."

"Oh that's a must, Ms. Langston," I said, as I held her car door open so that she could climb inside.

There was a brief silence between us as we looked into each other's eyes. I knew that I was on to something good with her and I wholeheartedly believed that she felt the same way about me.

20

Walter

Stretched out on the rear seat of Ethan's truck, I was on my phone checking my emails while we made our way to Memorial Drive. He had already picked up Greg, who was reclined in the passenger seat. The three of us were headed to Dugan's Tavern when Ethan looked back over his shoulder at me and asked, "You have enough room back there?"

"Of course, man," I replied, ignoring his sarcastic tone because I knew what was coming next.

There was more than enough room for me on the black leather bench seat. He already knew this, but as usual, he was giving me grief about my size.

"I'm just asking, dude," Ethan said with that goofy smile of his spreading across his face. "I know that seat's large enough for three adults, but I wasn't sure if it could accommodate all of you."

"Whatever, man. Your girl wasn't sure she could accommodate all of me either. But I taught her what it's like to be with a real man after I opened that thing up like a speculum," I said, reaching up to swat the back of his head.

"OOOOHHHH!" Greg yelled, putting his fist up to cover his mouth and burst into laughter.

"Nice one, big boy!" Ethan said, nodding in appreciation while he rubbed his head where I had popped him.

"Screw this," I said. "If this is how tonight's going to be, you can just turn this bucket around and take me back to the house. I can watch the game in peace by myself."

"C'mon, man," Greg said, turning to look back at me. "You know we're just messing with you."

"Yeah, man," Ethan added. "Don't get your ovaries twisted. You know we're going to tease you because it's been so long since you've gotten permission to go out with us. And what did you mean with that, 'by yourself', comment?"

I ignored his question, looking out the window in silence and took in the scenery passing by.

"What's up with you and that gargoyl...I mean girlfriend of yours?" he pressed. "You did tell her you're going out tonight, right? And watch what you're calling a bucket, too. Don't think I missed that."

"Whatever, man. We're good, okay?" I said, hoping that he would leave the subject alone.

I had not told anyone except Stacey about my conversation with Darlene, and that I had finally ended things with her. I don't know why I even told Stacey about my relationship with Darlene. We were just talking and the next thing I knew, I just opened up and told her my whole story.

It has been four days since I told Darlene that she would have to find her own place. When I followed up with her about this yesterday, she told me that she had checked a few places. I got the feeling she was dragging out the process with the belief that I would come to my senses.

I reiterated that she would have to move out. We ended up getting into a huge argument. She was saying that it wasn't right that she had to move out since I was the one that was breaking up with her. Since I was supposed to be the man, then I should pack my things and leave. I explained to her that the lease for the apartment, which was in my name, would be up in two months and I would be moving as soon as I closed on my new house. It didn't make sense for me to move just to have to turn around and move again. I told her that I didn't want to spend the next few months living in an apartment with my ex-girlfriend. We were over, she had to leave, and that was the end of the discussion.

Soon enough, Darlene would see that I was dead serious about what I wanted. By the end of the weekend, she would need to have made a decision on where she was going to live. It didn't matter where she chose, but she definitely would not be living with me.

My mind drifted to my conversation with Stacey yesterday. She was so appreciative of the flowers that I sent her. When I called her after my meeting, our conversation lasted for almost two hours as we talked about all kinds of things, including me and Darlene breaking up.

"I broke up with her," I said to Ethan, my mind returning to the present. "We're finished. Done. Over. Fini. All that. We...I mean 'I' ended things with Darlene."

"Ended things, huh?" Ethan said, looking over at Greg with a knowing expression.

"So what was it that all of a sudden made you come to the decision to end it with her? I've been telling you for years to let that controlling ass chick go and you never listened. Now all out the blue you're finally giving her the boot?"

"Man, there wasn't any one thing in particular, okay," I answered defensively. "I realized that things weren't working between us. I'd known this for a while. And yes, I know that you've been trying to tell me this. I had to come to this on my own though. And I did. End of story."

"So Stacey has nothing to do with it?" Ethan pressed. "She's got absolutely nothing to do with the fact that in less than a week, you're breaking up with this chick that you've been living with for the past year and have been dating for the past two years?"

I thought about his question before I answered him. He was right in that I was moving quickly, but this was something I should have done a long time ago.

"I'm not going to say all that," I said finally. "The fact remains that Darlene and I are through. That's all that matters. She's still staying at my crib until she moves into her spot and that's it. She's in the bedroom and I'm sleeping on the couch."

"Until she gets her own spot? And what damn couch on the planet could support your big ass?" Ethan said skeptically. "Anyway, I've heard that before. She's going to turn a few weeks of apartment hunting into a few months. That's going to turn into y'all ending up getting back together. She's going to wear you down, bro. Mark my words. As muscle bound as your physical body is, you are weak as hell when it comes to the heart. She knows this, and even worse, knows how to play you like a drum."

"Walter, I gotta agree," Greg interjected. He had been silent until then, but he took this opportunity to enter the conversation. "If you are serious, you have to set a hard and fast deadline. If not, she'll string things along, wear you down, and next thing you know, y'all will be married with kids living up in Cobb County somewhere. Women can be some devious creatures and Darlene's not going to go out quietly.

"The few times I've had the pleasure of having to interact with her," he continued, "she gave me the craziest vibe. I don't know how you did it, but I'm glad I didn't have to deal with her. If you broke it off with her then you need to tell her to go. And I mean sooner rather than later."

"I hear you, man," I said, turning to look out of the window.

"I've set things in motion,' I said quietly. "I'm following through on them. This weekend, she's going to sign a lease somewhere. I don't know where yet, but when I get home tonight, I'm going to let her know that by the end of the month, she's got to be gone."

"Damn, you're serious, huh?" Ethan said.

"Yeah. I'm dead serious," I said firmly, laying my head back against the headrest and closing my eyes.

We rode in silence the rest of the way to the sports bar, each of us caught up in our own thoughts.

My love life was going to be what it was. I finally knew where I wanted to be and it was time that I took control of things and do what had to be done. Regardless of what the catalyst was, I was confident that I was finally making the right moves.

21

Angel

*S*till reeling from the twists and turns of another episode of my favorite television show, I reached over to grab the remote control and turned off the television. Every Thursday night, I would tune in to see what drama the classy and intelligent mocha-skinned Washington DC 'fixer' would be getting herself into.

Ever since Stacey turned me on to the show, I would make sure that my schedule was free for that hour so I could sip a few glasses of wine as I got wrapped up in the latest episode.

"Wow! Shonda did it again," I said, referring to the talented writer and producer of the show. My heart was still pounding in my chest as I closed my laptop after I finished typing a post about the episode on my Facebook page.

I was heading into the kitchen to put my wine glass in the sink when my cell phone began ringing.

Looking at the caller ID, I saw that it was my friend calling.

Perfect timing, I thought as I picked up the phone. If he had called any earlier, I would have had no choice but to send him to voicemail. As much as I cared about him, I was not about to miss any of the show, especially the last few minutes because they were always the most suspenseful.

"Hey, baby," I said, answering the phone.

"Wassup, sexy," he said. There was a lot of background noise and it was a little difficult to hear him.

"Where are you?" I asked. "I can hardly hear you."

"Out with the fellas," he said. "Yeah, it's kind of loud in here. I'll go outside so you can hear me better. I was going to call you earlier, but I knew you'd be watching that chick flick of a TV show so I waited until it went off."

"I've told you a thousand times that my show is not a chick flick, thank you," I said, laughing. He tried watching it with me once and was in absolute torture. He could not get into it and just did not understand why everyone loved the show.

"Anyway, what's going on?" I asked.

"I had to call you because…hold on for a second," he said.

"What is it?" I asked, my curiosity growing.

The noise level in the background dropped dramatically so I knew that he had gotten somewhere quieter.

"Sorry about that. I had to go outside. There wasn't anywhere quiet inside there," he said. "Well, I had to call you because…I know we're supposed to be going out tomorrow, right?"

"Yes," I said. "You said you were going to take me out to the movies and then to Pappadeaux. We're still going, right?"

"Yes…and no," he said, taking a deep breath. "The truth of the matter is that…I can't afford to take you…to take you there. That's just not in my budget. I'm sorry. I thought I could swing it, but the truth is I can't. Not this week, anyway."

"What do you mean?" I asked, my anger beginning to rise. I could not believe this. He told me that we were going out and now he was backing out of our date at the last minute.

"You know I get paid every two weeks and I don't get paid again until next week. We can go out next weekend with no problem. I just can't do it this weekend."

This is truly ridiculous. Was I asking too much to expect that the man that I cared about, the man that supposedly cared about me, would be able to take me out to a nice restaurant without having to plan it four and five months in advance? I wasn't asking him to take me on a lavish vacation to Dubai for crying out loud.

"I should be getting a pretty good check next Friday," he continued. "I finished up a few big jobs and put in a lot of overtime last week. I also have a few side jobs coming up so I'll be getting paid for those as well. With all that, we can go out next weekend with no worries."

"Wait a minute," I said, seething at this whole change of events. "Aren't you out now? How come you can go out tonight and spend money but you've got to wait a whole week before you can take me out?"

There was silence on the phone for a few seconds before he spoke.

"Angel," he said quietly. "I'm not paying for anything tonight. My homeboy is paying because I did some work on his mom's car. We're just hanging out and he's picking up my tab, okay? We're friends and that's what we do. I haven't spent a dime tonight."

I was caught off guard at this. I was still angry at the situation and felt that I didn't deserve this, but I didn't have a good counter-argument.

"What about Saturday?" I asked, trying a different tack. "Or even Sunday? Couldn't we go out then instead?"

"No, because I won't have enough money at all this weekend," he said quietly.

"Couldn't you borrow some money from one of your so-called friends," I snapped, my frustration boiling over. "Don't you have a credit card? Just charge it this week and then pay the bill next week when you get the money you supposedly will get."

"Angel, I'm not going to do either of those," he said, an edge creeping into his tone. "Yes, I could borrow the money. Yes, I have a credit card. Man, I really wasn't expecting you to react like this."

"Well...because this isn't right," I said, trying weakly to defend myself. "I had my weekend planned with you based on you telling me that we were going out tomorrow. You planted the idea in my mind and now you're completely changing things."

"I'm not changing anything. I'm only postponing us going out, that's all. We can still spend time together, Angel," he said. "We can go to the movies this weekend if you like. Next Saturday, we can go out and do it big without me having to borrow from my friends or creditors. How about that?"

"Sure. Whatever," I said sullenly. "That's fine."

"Cool. I know you're disappointed, but it'll be fine, I promise," he said.

"Sure. I guess," I said dryly. "Okay. Well, I'm going to get ready for bed. I'll talk to you later," I said and hung up.

I was so upset with him. I have been wanting us to go out together for so long, and when he finally asks me out, he calls the very next day to say that he can't afford to take me where I want to go. Is this how it would be if he and I were to become a real couple?

Oh, well. I guess next Saturday will be fine, I thought as I went into the kitchen, slowly beginning to calm down. The warm, sudsy water running over my hands as I washed my wine glass and snack plate was soothing and helped to further relax me. As I rinsed out the glass and reached over to put it on the rack to dry, it hit me: I was going to the concert with Cory next Saturday.

22

Stacey

I thanked the valet as I took the parking ticket from him and put it along with my phone inside my purse. I stopped and used the reflective shine of the restaurant's large picture window by the front door to check my hair and make-up before walking through the entrance.

I checked my watch and saw that I was five minutes early for my lunch meeting with the prospective client who had asked to meet with me this afternoon. I had just received a text reply from her telling me that she was already in the restaurant and where she was located while she was waiting for me, so I was glad that I was on time and would not have to make her wait.

I went over to the table where she was seated and extended my hand to her.

At first glance, I saw that she was a beautiful woman. Her hair was professionally done in a fashionable style that accentuated the lines of her face. She had a slim, toned body and was dressed in a well-tailored, grey pant suit that was both flattering and professional.

"It's a pleasure to meet you," I said, extending my hand in greeting.

She wordlessly looked me up and down for a long while, as if sizing me up, taking a slow sip of the amber liquid in the glass that she casually held in her right hand. An uncomfortable silence lingered between us as she took her time draining the contents before putting the now empty glass on the table in front of her. She finally took my hand in hers and gave it a curt shake.

"I'm sure," she said dryly, shifting in her seat in order to cross her long legs at the knees.

I was a bit taken aback by her somewhat rude behavior, but decided to chalk it up as a weird personality quirk and get this over with. In my years of being a real estate agent, both with nationally recognized agencies and with my own company, I have come across all types of people. I have learned to take each individual personality that I encounter in stride and do what it takes to close the deal.

This particular client, who only referred to herself as 'Mrs. Johnson', had contacted me this morning and asked, better yet, demanded a meeting with me. I usually preferred meeting new clients in my office and only in certain circumstances did I make exceptions. She told me she had to leave out of town on a business trip and would be gone for a while. Compared to most Fridays, my calendar was free so I conceded to meeting with her at Sparcs restaurant.

"So, Mrs. Johnson," I said, focusing on the reason for the meeting and getting right down to business. "I really didn't get much information from you in our conversation earlier. As I tried to explain, I usually conduct a phone interview before meeting with my clients. That's to make sure I get a full understanding as to what you're searching for."

She continued to study me in silence for several moments before she took a tiny sip of the water that our server had just placed on the table in front of her.

"Actually," she said as she put the glass back on the table and daintily plucked a piece of lint off her pant leg with her manicured fingernails. "My fiancé has already been in contact with you about finding our new home. My husband-to-be is a very predictable man, so when he began to make dramatic changes in his behavior that were completely out of his character, I couldn't figure out why. I sat and thought about it and suddenly realized that all of this started when he went to look at houses a few weekends ago. And interestingly, that's coincidentally the same time that he met you. So with all of that, I took this meeting to see for myself just who was trying to interject herself into our lives."

I was stunned by her words which were delivered in a cold, steady tone that barely masked her contempt. I took a sip of my own water to give my heart a chance to stop pounding and hopefully give my brain a chance to catch up.

"Your fiancé? Who's your fiancé? I don't know who you're talking about," I said.

"Oh, please." She sneered. "You know exactly who my fiancé is so don't try to play innocent with me."

"I don't know your fiancé," I said, beginning to get irritated with her and whoever it was she was talking about. "Look, I don't know what's going on here. I don't know you or your fiancé, Mrs. Johnso…" I said, but at that moment, it hit me. As soon as I started to say her name along with the mention of showing houses last weekend, all of the pieces fell into place as I realized exactly who her fiancé was.

"Yes. That's right. You do know who he is," she said with a satisfied smile at the stunned expression of recognition that was written all over my face.

"Walter's my fiancé," she said, making sure to add extra emphasis on the word, 'my'. "Don't try to act like you didn't know." She smirked. "We've been engaged for a while now. In fact, the wedding is going to be in the Spring. We were thinking about having it in April."

I closed my eyes as the pain of her words made my very insides crumble. I thought about the times that Walter and I had spoken to each other. Not once did he mention anything about an engagement. He told me about his ex, Darlene, but what she was saying now didn't sound anything like the situation that he had explained to me.

This messy saga unfolding in front of me was exactly why I did not fool with married men, engaged men, or even men who had girlfriends. I knew the drama that came with men in those situations, so I made sure to keep all that foolishness away from my life.

I was getting angrier with each passing moment. I could not believe that I was in a nice restaurant playing out a scene from the latest ratchet reality show where otherwise mature women end up looking like hood rats fighting and cursing at each other over some worthless scrub of a man while he sat back laughing at their antics.

"If you like, I can put you on the guest list," she added, trying to push the emotional dagger in even deeper.

"So you must be Darlene," I said weakly, slumping down in my chair. I could not bring myself to look directly into her eyes. The humiliation that I felt was so powerful that it took all my fortitude to stay seated instead of getting up and running out the restaurant.

"That's right, I'm Darlene. So you know who I am yet you still continue to try and steal my man. Pathetic!" she spat.

"Wait a minute! It's not like that. He told me that y'all had broken up. I didn't know that he was still with you. I definitely didn't know that he was engaged. He said that y'all weren't together anymore," I said, trying weakly to protest. I was so taken off guard that my usual strength was totally gone.

"It's not like that? Still with me? Broken up?" she asked, her voice rising with each question that she threw at me. "You know what? It doesn't even matter. I want you to shut the hell up and listen! I found your business card in Walter's pocket. I checked his phone records and saw how much you and him have been communicating with each other. I know all about you and him and this...whatever the hell you think you have going on with my man. You better believe it ends now!"

She quickly got to her feet and stood over me, her fists clenched into tight balls at her side as her rage was barely under control.

Extending her index finger and pointing it a few inches from my nose, she screamed, "You think you're going to steal my man from me? You better think again if you believe that I'm just going to sit back and let that happen. Walter is my damn man and nobody, and I mean NOBODY, is going to take him from me. Stay the hell away from my fiancé!"

Slamming her palm down on the table to emphasize her point, she continued staring at me with pure hatred in her eyes before turning and walking out of the restaurant. The restaurant was not completely filled, but all of the twenty or so patrons were staring at me with obvious expressions of disgust on their faces. My shame grew even more intense as I picked up my purse and tried to make a hasty retreat out of the restaurant.

Once outside, I took several gulps of fresh air to try and calm my nerves. I could not believe what just happened. *How did I let myself get caught up in this mess?* I thought over and over again. Up until now, I had never romantically dealt with any man that was attached in any way to another woman. I never wanted to be the other woman and I knew that if a man cheated with me, then sooner or later, he would cheat on me.

I honestly thought Walter was better than that. I honestly thought he was one of the few good men left in the ever-shrinking pool of dateable men. Sadly, I realized that he was just like all of the others that I seemed to keep running into.

Having gathered myself, I walked to the valet stand and presented my claim ticket. As the valet ran off to retrieve my car, I looked around and saw Darlene sitting in her silver Lexus sedan parked across the street, staring at me. The moment we made eye contact, Darlene threw her head back and laughed before she sped off, tires squealing.

I had no idea what I had gotten myself into, but my building anger at having been played by Walter grew even greater.

As if on cue, my cell rung and without even having to look at the display, I knew that it was him. I glared at the phone before sending the call straight to voicemail.

I thanked the valet as he held my car door open. I climbed inside and as soon as the door was closed and I was safely behind the dark tint of my windows, the tears began to flow. I furiously pounded on the steering wheel, the anger, frustration and disappointment exploding out of me with each blow.

23

Walter

*M*oving day was thankfully here. It was only a few short weeks ago that I had told Darlene she had to move out. Finally, the day had come.

It was the perfect Saturday for moving. I could not wait to get Darlene out of my place and into her own apartment so I could enjoy the rest of the day, and more importantly, the rest of my life.

Ever since I told her that we were over and that she had to leave, she had been dragging her feet in looking for her own place. After my night out with Ethan and Greg, as soon as I got home, I told her in no uncertain terms that we were finished and insisted that she needed to begin looking for her own place.

It was only then that she reluctantly accepted my offer to help her find a place for her to live. I took her to visit several different apartment complexes that I found from online searches, but she wasn't satisfied with any of them. Using one absurd excuse or another, she refused to choose any of the places that we visited.

I remembered one of my past clients that was the property manager for a complex in the Perimeter Center area. I dug his business card out of my Rolodex and gave him a call to set things up. I took Darlene to visit the model units, and was both shocked and relieved when she settled on a spacious townhouse there.

She had made arrangements for one of her girlfriends, Veronica, to be her roommate. They had already signed the lease; however, Veronica would not be moving in for two weeks since she was out of town on a business trip.

Darlene had wanted to wait to leave my place so that she could move in at the same time as her new roommate. I did something that I did not do enough of during our time together—I stood my ground and told Darlene no. I told her that she had signed the lease, so there was no reason for her to stay with me any longer. She was moving out this weekend and that was not going to change.

She stared at me with a mixture of surprise and hatred before grabbing her purse and keys and storming out the apartment. I peered out the window and watched as her car screeched out the parking lot. I didn't know where she was going, nor did I care. I went to the kitchen, pulled out the bottle of pineapple rum that was tucked in the refrigerator door, mixed it with some Sprite, and sat on the couch to enjoy the moment. I sipped my drink in the peaceful silence, counting the days until it was time for her to move.

Now here we were, finally, doing something that I should have done a long time ago. *Only a few more miles,* I thought as I checked the mirrors and carefully changed lanes as I maneuvered the big twenty foot U-Haul truck that I had picked up yesterday to make sure that everything was in place for Darlene's move.

It took Ethan, his brother, Evan, and me over two hours to load all of Darlene's stuff into the truck. I was glad that my friend had come through to help. I was really reluctant to ask him, but when I did, he said he would be there. Knowing him, he probably just wanted to see for himself that Darlene was really moving out. Whatever his motivations, he and Evan were there helping me so I was not complaining.

For the past two days she had been boxing up all of her things. She had not said anything to me as she stuffed her belongings in to the large cardboard boxes. I offered several times to help, but her vicious glare signaled that she did not want my assistance.

When it was all said and done, Darlene had twice as much stuff as I did. It seemed that during our time together, I really hadn't acquired anything of any real personal value. I was shocked to see that everything that belonged to me could probably easily have fit into one average-sized room. Whereas all of my clothes and belongings could fit into the bed of a pick-up truck, we needed one of the larger moving trucks to pack all of her things.

I looked in the mirror to see how far Ethan was behind us. As annoying as he can be at times, there is no doubt that he is my friend. He and his younger brother showed up right on time and between the three of us, we quickly knocked out the loading of the truck. It was even better that Ethan had a full-sized pickup truck because we were able to throw a few of the smaller, more fragile items in the truck bed.

Ethan was not his usual joking self today. In fact, he was rather subdued the entire morning, quietly going about the task of loading the truck without his usual inane banter. At one point, I pulled his brother aside and asked him what was up with Ethan. Evan just shrugged his shoulders. Neither of us could figure out what was going on so we let him be and rolled with it.

I glanced over at Darlene who was riding shotgun in the cab with me. Why she chose to ride in the truck as opposed to taking her own car was beyond me. Maybe she thought there was a chance that she could convince me to change my mind and for us to stay together, but there was no way that was going to happen. Our relationship was over, and more importantly, I was going to pursue someone who I believed would make me happy.

The evening before, I had called Stacey. I wanted to share with her that Darlene would be moving out today but I never got the chance to do so. I tried to tell her about this major step in my life, however she seemed to be a bit distant. The happiness that was usually in her voice was not there. In fact, she seemed angry with me for some reason. I wasn't sure what was going on or if I had done something wrong, so I told her that I would talk to her later and ended the call. I was truly puzzled by her behavior but I didn't dwell on this for too long. I was too caught up in the feeling of happiness from the thought of Darlene being gone and how bright the future was looking.

I thought about the differences between Stacey and Darlene being like night and day. I tried to never compared the two women but there were times when it was impossible not to do so. Stacey was such a genuinely good person. I felt so good, so easy, every time I spoke to her. Darlene was like a rich cheesecake—good in small doses but too much of her made you sick to your stomach.

"So, how do you feel?" I asked Darlene, trying to break the silence. I knew it was a ridiculously silly question, but I was grasping at straws hoping we could have a decent conversation to at least try and pass the time. I was holding out all hope that we could at least have some sort of friendship when it was all said and done.

Darlene snapped her head around and gave me the coldest look. She stared directly at me without saying anything for a good ten seconds. I tried to hold her disconcerting gaze, but I had to avert my eyes, both to keep us safely on the road, but more so because her intense look was actually physically painful.

A few minutes passed before I decided to try again. "So how are you going to get your car? I don't understand why you left it behind when you could have driven it yourself,"

"Don't worry about my car. In fact, don't say anything to me," she said through clenched teeth. "I hate you so much right now. You think I haven't noticed how you've been acting lately. How you've been walking around with that stupid ass smile on your face. I know what you've been up to. I know you have somebody else. You're only supposed to love me. Only me! Instead you're trying to throw me out of your life like I'm a stinking bag of trash."

I was blown away by how angry she was. I knew that she was upset with how things between us had turned out but I did not know her feelings were so intense.

"I'm sorry you feel that way," I said. "I do love you though, Darlene. Why do you think that I've been trying to help you throughout all of this? Whether you believe me or not, I want what's best for you. I just know that what we had wasn't working. I did what I felt was the best thing for me and for us."

"Go to hell!" She hissed. "Don't give me that mess. You just met somebody else and decided you didn't want me anymore. It's not going to be that easy though. Trust me on that."

It's not going to be that easy? I thought as I looked at her out of the corner of my eye. I tried to read her face and body language, hoping to pick up a clue as to what she meant. Her angry visage didn't reveal much beyond the obvious fury that was burning inside her.

"What do you mean by that, Darlene?" I asked, hoping that she would cool down and explain.

"Just shut the hell up and don't say anything else to me," she snapped.

I could feel the heat coming from her, radiating in the confined space of the small cab of the truck, her anger raging like an inferno. I knew there was nothing more I could say or do, so I decided to respect her wish and said nothing else to her, focusing my attention on the road ahead.

We rode in silence for the rest of the trip to her new apartment. I was so happy that she would soon be moved into her own place and this chapter of my life would soon be over.

24

Ethan

*W*e were driving in light traffic, following Walter and Darlene. The U-Haul truck was a few car lengths in front of us and we were going at a slow, easy pace. I had the cruise control set to match the U-Haul's speed, but par for the course when it came to driving in Atlanta, cars were passing us on both sides like we were virtually standing still.

The sky overhead was clear and the crisp fall air flowing through the truck's partially lowered windows was cool and pleasant.

"What's on your mind, man?" Evan asked, looking over at me from the passenger seat.

I came back to reality and looked over at him, shaking my head. We had been riding along in relative silence from the moment we left Walter's apartment fifteen minutes ago.

"Nothing much. Just thinking," I responded soberly.

"You sure? You don't seem to be yourself today," he said.

I looked over at my younger brother and smiled at his concern. He and I were very different but yet so alike in many ways. He was a quiet, driven man who was seven years younger than me. The owner of one of Atlanta's premier custom car and home audio installation shops, he had done jobs for some of the A-list celebrities throughout the metro area. I was so proud of him and all that he had accomplished.

"I'm good, little bro," I said, returning my attention to the road.

"I was thinking about my boys. Walter. Greg. You. All of y'all," I said. "Walter's taking some big steps, man. Not only breaking up with Darlene, but moving her out so that he can move on with his life. That's a really big deal. I honestly never thought he'd do this because of how passive he can be when it comes to her.

"And Greg," I continued. "I don't know what's going on with him. He was supposed to be helping us out today but he called this morning and said he wouldn't be able to make it. He didn't say why or anything else beyond that."

I paused, looked at him for a few seconds before continuing. "And you, my man. It's been a minute since we hung out together. I know you're doing your thing. I saw your feature in *Auto Audio* magazine, by the way. I'm proud of you, man," I said as I reached over to pat him on his shoulder.

"I appreciate that, man," was all he said in his low-key way as he accepted my praise.

We settled back into silence and listened to the up-tempo music from the local hip-hop radio station. As we passed the Chamblee-Dunwoody exit, Walter put on the U-Haul's turn signal and started moving into the right lane so that he could exit on to Ashford-Dunwoody road.

"Almost there," I said, following Walter on to the exit ramp. "I want to hurry up and get this over with as quickly as possible."

A few more turns and we were pulling into a luxury apartment complex. At first glance, I instantly knew it was that filled with all of the high-end comforts needed to keep Darlene satisfied.

We followed Walter as he carefully navigated through the complex until he pulled in front of the correct building. He slowly backed the U-Haul up to the building's entrance, parked, and climbed out of the truck.

I then backed my truck into the space beside the U-Haul, got out and walked over to Walter and Darlene.

"This is really nice, Darlene," I said, looking around at the large property's lush, manicured landscaping.

"And look over there," I continued, pointing at the numbered, covered spaces across the parking lot from where we were standing. "You've got a place where you can park your broom and not have to worry about it getting wet when it rains."

She whirled around and lunged at me but Walter stepped between us and caught her just before she could plunge her talons into my flesh.

"You motherfu—" she shrieked as Walter did his best to restrain her.

161

"Whoa! Whoa!" He said as he carried her away from us, literally kicking and screaming.

"Ethan, please don't. This is going to be difficult enough. Please don't make it any harder than we have to. Please," Walter pleaded over his shoulder, using his body to separate the two of us.

"Okay, okay," I said, holding my hands up in surrender and backing away from them.

"You stupid, you know that, right?" Evan said, shaking his head and chuckling as he went to the back of the U-Haul to open it up.

We spent the next few hours unloading both trucks. After making sure everything was placed exactly where Darlene wanted it, Evan and I went down to the truck to leave Walter alone with her.

"Thanks for helping out. You can take my truck back and get your car. Just leave the keys in the house and lock the door behind you. I'll ride back with Walter and get in with his spare key," I said as I tossed Evan the keys.

"Alright, cool. I'll catch up with you," he said and gave me a brotherly hug.

Climbing into the now empty cargo compartment of the truck, I stretched out and relaxed, scrolling through my Facebook timeline as I waited for Walter.

"You straight?" I asked when he finally came down and we both climbed into the cab of the truck.

"Yeah, I'm good," he said as he started the truck with a loud rumble and pulled out of the parking lot. "Relieved actually. I tried to talk to her but she's so mad. I've never seen her like this. It was kind of scary to be honest."

I looked over at him and saw that he was genuinely shook up.

"It's going to be alright, man. She'll be fine," I said, trying to get him to relax. "This is all kind of sudden for her so she's going to need some time to absorb everything."

"But her anger, though," he said, shaking his head. "I know things might have happened quickly but her anger level is off the charts."

"Seriously?" I said, glancing over at him, surprised at how visibly shaken he was. I wasn't quite sure what to make of this, so I decided to say nothing. We rode in silence for a few miles before Walter spoke again.

"What are you doing tonight?" he asked suddenly.

"Why? You trying to take me out? Is that the real reason why you moved Darlene out?"

"Whatever, fool," he responded, laughing. "I just want to take you and Evan out somewhere to say thanks for helping me out today."

"Yeah, that's cool," I said. "There's going to be plenty to get into tonight so that's right on time. I'll do the flying since you're buying."

"No doubt. I didn't feel like driving and dealing with the traffic tonight anyway. Thanks, man," he said before turning his head to look at the road ahead, returning to his thoughts.

25

Angel

The doorbell began to chime right as I was applying the final touches to my make-up. I took one last look in the bathroom mirror and finished up before going over to peek through the curtains by my front door.

As expected, it was Cory coming to pick me up, standing there with a beautiful bouquet of flowers. I appreciated his punctuality and the flowers were an extra treat. It seemed like most guys I dated lately felt that being forty-five minutes late to pick me up was no big deal. And, to add insult to injury, they would show up empty-handed. I had to give him kudos, because he was really off to a good start.

Damn! He looks good, I thought, taking another few seconds to check him out through the curtains. As usual, the man was the epitome of fashion. He was dressed casually for the evening in a camel hair sport coat over a sea foam green oxford shirt, well-fitting dress jeans, and tan loafers that perfectly matched the color of the stylish coat. *Mm mm mmm,* I thought, supressing a smile a I opened the door to greet him.

Our evening together went even better than I could have expected. As the lights came up to signal the end of the show, everyone in the audience stood to their feet to give a standing ovation. Not only was Maxwell a talented singer, he also put on one hell of a performance. Of the many concerts that I had been to in Atlanta, this was one of the best that I had attended.

"Oh my God! That was great!" I gushed, barely able to contain my excitement.

"I agree. That was a really good show," he replied with equal enthusiasm." And the seats made the show even better. I've got to email my man and tell him thanks for giving them to me. Hell, as good as those tickets were, I might even send him a bottle of wine or something as a token of appreciation."

"That's a good idea," I said.

I was impressed with everything about Cory so far and was more than pleasantly surprised at how well the evening was going. Once again, I was kicking myself for not going out with him sooner.

"So, what would you like to do now?" Cory asked as we made our way outside along with the thousands of other concertgoers who had been packed inside the theater for the sold out show.

"I'm not sure," I responded. "Did you have anything in mind?"

"I have a few ideas," he said cheerily. "But the night's still young. It's only ten-fifteen so I know there's still plenty to get into."

"That's true," I said noncommittally.

I knew that I made the right decision to go out with Cory; however, I still felt bad for brushing my friend off at the last minute. As much as I had enjoyed myself tonight, and even though I tried not to, my mind kept drifting off to my friend. Time and time again, I found myself wondering where he was and what he was doing.

The crisp, cool night air was a dramatic contrast to the warm theater as we walked up Peachtree Street to the parking lot where Cory had parked his black BMW 640i sports coupe. The ride from my loft in the East Lake area of Atlanta to the Fox Theater downtown was an absolute dream. Nestled in the butter soft leather seats, we seemingly floated through the streets of Atlanta.

This car was an example of the luxury that I felt I should be surrounded with. Cory was the exact kind of man that I wanted to be with because I knew he could provide me with all the things that I wanted.

"Let's go grab something to eat," he said. "How does that sound?"

"Sounds good to me," I responded.

"Are you okay?" he asked, looking at me curiously.

"I'm fine," I responded quickly. "What makes you ask that?"

"Well, you seem a little distracted," he said, a strange look settling across his face. "You're a million miles away. Like the song says, 'Your body's here with me, but your mind's on the other side of town.' Is everything okay?"

I didn't realize I was being so transparent with my thoughts and behavior. He had said it jokingly, but I was still embarrassed that he picked up on the fact that my mind was indeed on the other side of town. I knew I had to control myself and focus on the evening at hand and not worry about anything or anyone else.

"Oh, I'm sorry, Cory," I said, plastering a huge smile on my face. "I was thinking about a conversation I had with the project manager on the Blue Ocean cologne advertising campaign. I'm really excited about that project. I guess I need to leave work at work."

"That's hard to do sometimes, right?" Cory said, his posture relaxing. "I'm excited about that account as well. My sales team really hustled to win that account. It can be hard to turn off work mode sometimes. I know it took me a while to do that. There were some times in the past where I regularly worked sixty hour weeks. It seemed like I would eat, sleep, and breathe work. The money's good, but my personal life suffered tremendously."

The serious tone that entered his voice as he made this last comment startled me a little. In that moment, I realized that I really didn't know anything about Cory. I knew him from work and the few minor details we had exchanged with each other in casual conversation, but the more I thought about it, I could not escape the fact that I didn't know anything about him.

I had to ask myself if I wanted to get to know him better. Did I want to keep our relationship on the level that it currently occupied, or did I want to take it further? I knew that Cory was very interested in me and because of this, I controlled the direction that our relationship would flow. I thought back to the BMW's comfortable seats and my decision was made for me.

"Really? How did your life suffer?" I asked, deciding to probe deeper, hoping he would share more with me.

"It cost me my wife and children, that's how," he said abruptly.

"Your wife? Children? You were married?" I blurted out, not able to control the shock at hearing these startling revelations.

Before now, the topic of him being married with children had never come up. He never mentioned having kids and the few times that I visited his office, there were no pictures of his family displayed anywhere. In fact, the more I thought about it, there were no personal touches to indicate anything other than his professional accomplishments. Besides the plaques which held his degrees and certifications, there were no photos of any kind to be found anywhere in his office.

I didn't have a problem with a man who was divorced, and I could even deal with a man with children. That was to be expected in this day and age. In my mind, there really weren't many reasons that a single man in my age group would never be married or at least have children. To me, that was suspect and warranted a closer look. Either he had kids and was not claiming them, or he was married but creeping around. The most nefarious was that he was secretly a member of the large population of down low gay men in Atlanta.

"I'd rather not talk about it," he said coldly.

"I really would like to know," I said, trying to take a soft approach, hoping this would get him to open up and reveal more about himself.

"What did I say?" he snapped. "I don't want to talk about that."

"Okay, okay. I'm sorry," I said, surprised by his sudden outburst.

This was a side of Cory that I had never seen. I looked over at him and saw that his normally handsome features were now shrouded with a mask of anger. First the revelation of him having kids or being married and now his current behavior. My mind was racing as I wondered what else about him was bubbling under the surface waiting to rear up and surprise me.

We walked in silence the rest of the way to the parking lot. The air between us was heavy with the weight of his disclosure.

As we approached his car, he took his iPhone out of his pocket. Using an app on the device, he remotely started the engine. For the second time that evening, instead of opening my door for me, Cory hit the button on the remote to unlock the doors and climbed in behind the steering wheel. I stood waiting at my car door, hoping that he would take the hint. Instead, he sat in the car, waiting for me to get in on the passenger side. He had done the same thing when he picked me up to begin our night out. It bothered me that he didn't take the time to open my door for me, but I looked past it. Considering how great the night had been up to this point, it really wasn't that big of a deal.

We sat silently in the car for a few tense seconds before he spoke.

"Don't ever push me like that again," he said flatly, his voice piercing the silent interior of the vehicle.

"I'm sorry," I repeated softly, looking over at him to try and gauge his emotions. He did not look as angry as he did earlier, but there was no denying his mood. He looked straight ahead through the windshield, his eyes sharply narrowed into slits. I didn't know what dark place me pushing him on the subject of his family had taken him, but I knew never to do that again. I turned and looked out my window at the lights of the buildings in downtown Atlanta.

"It won't happen again," I said softly.

"Good," he said, turning to look at me.

He shook his head and seemed to come out of his trance. Putting the car in gear, he slowly pulled out of the parking lot and carefully merged into traffic on Peachtree Street. The normally busy thoroughfare was even more so tonight as it seemed everyone in Atlanta was out and about, enjoying the pleasant fall weather.

"We're going to Buckhead," Cory said. "There's a nice restaurant over there I've been to before. It's only a few minutes away."

"That's fine," I said, sitting in the comfortable seat, stuck in the middle of an uncomfortable situation.

26

Ethan

After Walter dropped me off at home, I called Evan to tell him about Walter's plan to take us out to thank us for helping him move. Walter didn't really know where he wanted to go so he asked me to come up with a spot for the night and he would take care of the bill.

"I've called damn near everywhere. All of them are saying that they aren't taking any more reservations. It's crazy!" I said. I was sitting on the couch surfing websites still searching for a good place for us to go. There were so many events happening tonight that finding somewhere was proving to be a lot more difficult than I expected.

"Yeah, the city's going to be jumping, that's for sure," Evan said loudly, having to raise his voice above the high-pitched whine of whatever power tool that he was using.

"Man, what are you doing over there?" I asked.

"I'm in the lab putting the finishing touches on my latest client's project," he said before turning off the machine and speaking at a normal volume. "He's some new mumble rapper on the scene. I can't understand a damn thing he's saying but he's making money because he paid in cash. Up front. Didn't even negotiate when I gave him my price. Anyway, I used his deposit to buy a new router and I'm loving it."

"Oh, okay," I said. "How's the project looking?"

"So far, so good," he said. "But as far as heading out tonight, I'll tell you right now that I don't do lines. Give me a few minutes and I'll work it out,"

"Okay, bet," I said as I ended the call, smiling at the Lucas arrogance being in full effect.

I didn't know what he had up his sleeve but I knew my brother. He built his very successful business on the premise of, 'It's not what you know, but who you know.' He had an impressive list of contacts that had served him well over the past few years.

Not even ten minutes later, Evan called back to say that he had a solution to our situation.

"We're good to go," he said. I could just see the satisfied grin that I knew he had plastered on his face.

"Really? What did you come up with?" I asked, hitting the mute button on the television and sitting up on the couch.

"Check this out," he began, "About six weeks ago, I rewired a horrible theater room installation job in this mini-mansion over in Dunwoody. Not too far from where we were today, in fact. Anyway, dude liked my work so much that he had me install a custom audio system in his Land Rover. Well, it turns out that he's the general manager for Quip. He told me that if I ever wanted to fall through there, all I had to do is to call him. Well, I took him up on it and all we have to do tonight is be there at eight for the table that he has reserved for us."

"That's wassup!" I said.

"Like I told you, big bro, I don't do lines," he said confidently.

He gave me all the details, which I passed on to Walter. I asked Walter if it was cool that Greg rolled with us even though he never did show up to help with the moving. Walter didn't mind, so the plans were made.

Later that evening, I picked up both Greg and Walter, and we headed over to Quip, the trendy restaurant in the Buckhead area of Atlanta. Located in Phipps Plaza, an upscale mall in the wealthiest section of town, it was frequented by Atlanta's most affluent citizens. It was the go-to spot for sports figures, reality show stars, and everyone else in between.

We arrived at the restaurant right on time. After having the valet park my truck, we went straight inside. We walked right by the crowd of people at the door who were waiting for a table. Ignoring their jealous stares, we went inside and met up with Evan who was already seated at a high-top table.

For the last few minutes, I'd been telling the guys the story about one of my drivers who had been bragging about his latest girlfriend.

"Every time he came back to the yard," I said, "he'd go on and on about how fine she was. He kept on telling me about how she looked like Pinky, the porn star. So in my mind I'm thinking that even if she didn't have pink hair, at least she had Pinky's massive badonkadunk. Here's the thing though, whenever I asked him to show me a picture of her, he never had one. Nothing on his Facebook page, his phone. Nothing."

"C'mon, man!" Greg said upon hearing this. "You telling me that in this day of camera phones he didn't have a picture of her? Sounds like some ol' catfish stuff to me."

We all started laughing at this reference to the popular television show where people claimed to be something that they knew they were not.

"Exactly!" I said. "So anyway, I was at Southlake Mall in Jonesboro about two weeks ago and just happened to run into him and his lady friend. Man, this chick didn't look anything like Pinky. Her big ass looked more like Precious!"

The guys started cracking up with laughter and I had to join in as I remembered Dwayne squirming because he did not anticipate me running into them.

"Let me quit," I said as the laughter died down. "Honestly, she was a little on the heavy side, but she really wasn't un-pretty at all. In fact, she was a really nice, friendly woman. She's a nurse at the DeKalb Medical hospital on our side of town. What I don't get though is why he was lying about how she looked."

I took a sip of my drink and said, "Anyway, speaking of un-pretty women, congrats to Baby Nuts Herc over here. Can y'all believe that he broke up with that harpy disguised as Darlene and actually moved her out of his spot? I honestly never saw that coming but Lord knows it didn't come soon enough. Let's raise our glasses to Walter who now officially has both his testicles back. Umm...she did give them back, didn't she?"

"Whatever, Ethan," Walter said, laughing as he reached over and gave me a playful shove on the shoulder. "I want to thank y'all for helping me. I really appreciate you guys today."

"No doubt," Greg said, nodding his head in agreement and raising his Long Island Iced Tea. "I hate I couldn't come through and help you move," he continued. "I was out of it this morning. I had a lot of stuff on my mind. I thought that—"

Greg stopped talking and stared at something over my shoulder that had obviously caught his attention.

Walter and I had pushed our chairs aside and were standing with our backs to the door. Evan and Greg were in their seats, directly in front of us with their backs to the wall, positioned so that he could see everyone who was coming through the entrance. The restaurant had large picture windows which stretched across the front entrance, so they had a clear view of the patrons who were entering through the hostess station situated by the front door.

"Greg? You okay?" I asked, wondering what had made him stop talking so abruptly.

I turned around to try and see who or what had captured his attention. I looked around but didn't see anything except the large group of people milling around either waiting to be seated or for a seat to open up at the bar.

I scanned the crowd again and that's when I saw her standing by the entrance, looking over in our direction.

"Hey, that's Stacey's homegirl," I said, turning back to face the group.

"Stacey! Where?" Walter exclaimed, spitting out his drink with excitement as he swiveled his head trying to look around.

"Stacey's friend, man," I said to him, shaking my head. "Anyway, I don't know the guy that she's with, but it looks like they're trying to find a seat. That's not going to happen though because this place is packed."

"Mmm hmmm," Greg murmured in response. He still had that bewildered expression on his face as he continued to stare at the couple.

"I'm going to see if they want to sit with us," I said to the guys and started waving my arm to beckon them over.

"Hold on, man," Greg said suddenly, reaching out and grabbing my forearm to stop me. "Don't do that. They'll be okay. It looks like they're on a date or something anyway." He sneered, releasing my arm. "They probably wouldn't want to be bothered with me...I mean with us."

What the hell's wrong with him? I thought as I studied him closely. This did not make sense at all. Our table was one of the largest in our section so there was plenty of room for them to join us. I didn't see anything wrong with having her and her friend come over and sit with us.

"Do you know ol' boy she's with?" I asked, thinking that maybe Greg knew the guy and might have had a previous run-in with him. I knew Greg well enough to know that he wasn't one for social niceties with someone that he didn't care for.

"Nah. I don't," he answered in a clipped tone.

"Alright then," I responded. "I don't know what's going on, but they're already heading this way."

I glanced over at Walter and Evan to see if they had noticed the change in Greg's behavior, but I could tell that they were just as confused as I was.

I gave up trying to figure him out and instead walked over to greet Angel and her date and escort them over.

27

Angel

When we pulled into the restaurant's parking lot, Cory instantly grunted his displeasure. "Damn!" he said. "I can't believe this! Look how crowded it is."

He had remained quiet and withdrawn for most of the ride over here. I still wasn't sure why he had the reaction that he did. I wanted to ask him about it but thought better of it and just rode along in silence.

After a few minutes, he loosened up a little and the pleasant Cory that I was used to seeing came back. We were able to make small talk with each other which helped me to relax.

I was so glad that we had gotten past the tense mood earlier. I was hoping that this was a step in the right direction and hopefully he would open up even more when we got to the restaurant.

"Yeah, it's packed," I agreed. As I observed the mass of people standing in front of the restaurant trying to get inside, I knew that any type of intimate conversation tonight was out of the question.

"Well, we're here now, so we might as well check it out," he said as he pulled the car up to the valet station.

After leaving the keys with the valet, we walked past the outside patio seating area that was overflowing with people.

"Wow! This is crazy," Cory remarked as we walked to the front door.

As soon as he opened it, the volume coming from inside hit us full on. The sound of the energetic gathering reinforced the fact that there was a capacity crowd in the building tonight.

We made our way over to the hostess station to see if we could get lucky and maybe get a booth or a table.

"I'm sorry, but there's a two hour wait," she informed us with a sympathetic smile. "I'll be more than happy to put your name on the list if you'd like."

I was not surprised at the wait considering the long line of people who were also standing around trying to get in. Cory gave her his name before we stepped back outside to decide if we would wait at the bar or leave altogether and find another restaurant.

"Stay here," Cory said into my ear. He had to speak loudly in order to be heard over the mixture of music and conversation coming from inside the restaurant.

"I'm going to see if my buddy is working tonight," he said as he looked around the crowd. "He's a golfing partner of mine and one of the managers here."

I was looking at the crowd of people, all ages and races, packed into the large dining area. As my eyes travelled around the room, taking in the faces of everyone in the restaurant, all smiling and happy, obviously enjoying themselves, my heart stopped as soon as I saw him.

I could not believe it. He was there with three other guys all seated at a large table. He hadn't yet noticed me, but I saw him as if he was the only one in the building and was standing under a spotlight. He was dressed casually and was laughing with his buddies about something.

He was in the middle of saying something and was looking around the dining room at the same time. In that instant, his eyes met mine and locked. He stopped talking instantly, his face showing the surprise that was registered at my presence.

I'd told him that I would be with my girls so I knew he was wondering why I was standing there in the restaurant alone instead of being where I said I was going to be.

At that exact moment, Cory came back and stood in front of me, leaning in close so that he could be heard over the noisy restaurant.

"We might as well leave," he said, his lips so close that they were almost touching my ear. "My friend isn't working the kitchen tonight. There aren't any empty tables and the bar is jam packed. I'm not about to wait two hours for a table."

I looked past Cory and saw Greg's eyes widen with even more surprise at the fact that not only was I there, but I was not alone.

I felt a wave of relief wash over me because hopefully I would be getting out of this messed up situation soon. I needed to get out of here and have a chance to regroup and catch my breath. As big as metro Atlanta was, with over five and a half million people living within its six hundred and sixty square miles, why did we have to end up in the same place?

The sooner we could leave here, the better. I knew that I would have some serious explaining to do, but right about now, I wanted to get out of here as quickly as possible.

"Okay, that's fine. Let's go," I said, hoping that I did not sound too relieved.

Just when I thought my luck was turning, reality set in.

His buddy across from him must have noticed the expression on his face and the change in his body language. As if trying to figure out what was going on, he turned to see who his buddy was looking at. That's when Ethan noticed me standing there at the entrance.

A huge smile spread on his face when he recognized me. He instantly waved me over to come and join them.

I closed my eyes and dropped my head, all the while asking myself if tonight would get any worse.

Cory noticed him beckoning us over and asked me, "Do you know him?"

"Yes," I sighed, wondering how Cory was going to react. "I know him. That's one of Stacey's friends," I answered, trying to make sure that Cory would not think anything was going on between us.

"Oh, okay. Stacey? The real estate friend, right?" he asked. "Let's go sit with them."

"Are you sure?" I asked with evident hesitation, hoping I could change his mind. He seemed to be oblivious to my state of panic, and I knew that sooner or later, all hell would break loose if we went over to that table.

"Of course," he said as he took my elbow and led me through the crowded room over to their table. "There aren't any seats in here. It looks like they've got space at their table and he's obviously inviting us over, so why not?"

He stopped and pulled me close, forcing me to turn and look at him. "What is it? Is there something that I should know?" As I looked into his eyes and felt his grip on my elbow tighten ever so slightly, I knew he definitely was not joking when he asked this.

"What?" I said quickly, hoping that the look on my face did not reveal the truth. "No, he's just one of Stacey's friends. The other three guys are his brother and best friends. That's it. I promise," I said, trying to reassure him. "I just...I just wanted it to be me and you tonight, that's all."

"Oh, okay," he said, his mood relaxing, causing him to release the pressure on my elbow. "I did as well. We can do that another time. How about we go out again? Maybe next week we can go someplace a lot quieter and less crowded. Just me and you. How does that sound?"

"That sounds great," I said, trying to sound as enthusiastic as possible and touching him lightly on his arm. "Look, let's just go over there. If we don't, his arm might fall off if he keeps waving it any longer."

"Cool," Cory said with a satisfied smile.

I hope everything will be cool, I thought as I allowed Cory to lead me over to the table. I didn't know how things were going to play out tonight, but I knew that at least one person was going to get hurt, namely me.

28

Walter

We were heading home after what had to be one of the most interesting days of my life. "What a day," I said to no-one in particular as I sat in the back of Ethan's truck.

"Ain't that the truth," Ethan agreed dryly.

"Mmm hmm," Greg answered in that same distant tone that he had been using all night ever since Angel and her date, Cory, joined us at our table.

I didn't know what was going on between Angel and Greg, but something was definitely there. I could tell Ethan was just as curious as to what was going on as well.

We rode in silence, heading down a nearly deserted I-85, making our way to Lithonia to drop me off at my apartment. My mind drifted off, thinking about all kinds of random nothings before finally settling on Stacey. I could see her pretty face in my mind's eye and all I could think about was calling her when I got home.

Ethan suddenly reached over and turned down the radio.

"So how long have y'all two had something going on?" he asked, his sudden question catching both Greg and me by surprise.

"We don't have anything going on," I said.

"Say what?" Ethan asked in a tone dripping with both sarcasm and confusion.

I took a deep breath before I spoke, quietly saying, "We don't have anything going on, per se. I mean, ever since I met her, she's been on my mind. I want to get with her though, that's for sure. I mean, Stacey's gorgeous and smart and sexy and all that I think I want in a woman. I just had to end things with Darlene before I could even begin to try to pursue her."

The only sounds in the truck came from the radio where Charlie Wilson's cut "There Goes My Baby" was playing softly through the speakers.

"Man, what in the hell are you talking about?" Ethan yelled out, his voice booming through the quiet cab.

Greg recovered from being startled by Ethan's outburst and started shaking his head, chuckling to himself as he turned back to look out of his window.

"Huh? I thought you wanted to…" I said, confused as to what Ethan was talking about.

"Look man. I don't know who you think you're fooling because we all know you're digging Stacey," Ethan said, using a voice that one would use if they were trying to explain a complicated math problem to a first grader.

"Real talk," he continued, "I hope y'all two can get together. You don't know how happy I am that you finally got rid of Darlene. I have to applaud you for finally moving her out of your spot and hopefully out of your life. All that being said and done, however, I wasn't talking to you. This cat sitting beside me knows I was talking to him," he said, gesturing at Greg with his thumb.

"Whatever, Ethan. Leave it alone, man," Greg said without turning his head to look at Ethan.

"Nah, bruh. I can't do that," Ethan replied adamantly as he exited off I-85 and merged unto I-20.

"I know something's up, I just don't know what exactly. How long has it been going on?" he asked again.

I sat up in my seat, listening to the conversation. I had known Ethan for a long while, but I really didn't know Greg that well. We were cool with each other, but our only interactions were through Ethan as he was the common bond between us. There was no doubt that Ethan and Greg were close friends as Greg had been the best man at Ethan's wedding. I could understand why Ethan was so upset that Greg kept such a big secret from him.

I decided that the best thing to do was be quiet and listen.

"Damn, Ethan. Leave it alone, man," Greg repeated, raising his voice and snapping his head away from the window to face Ethan.

He was obviously starting to get annoyed, but this did not seem to faze Ethan in the least.

"Bruh, you can put all the bass you want in your voice. That mess don't bother me," Ethan said with a smirk. "So, what's going on with y'all, man?"

Greg shrugged and turned to look out the window, shaking his head, resigned to the fact that Ethan was not going to let it go.

Both Greg and I knew that Ethan would not let anything rest. He was like a pit bull when he latched on to something. No matter how aggressive Ethan could be, the bottom line was that he was our friend and only wanted the best for us.

Greg turned from the window, blew out a long breath, and began speaking. "We've been seeing each other for a few months now. You know me, man. I've been with a lot of women and you know how that's gone. I play them and I've been played. I thought that's the way things were going to be for me until I met her. Hell, you were there when I met her, remember?"

"You mean at Dannette's fight party?" Ethan asked.

"Yep, that's it," Greg said. "The one back in April. That's when Stacey introduced me to Angel."

"Hold up," I yelled, interrupting their conversation. "What fight party? Why didn't you tell me about that, Ethan? Why wasn't I invited?"

Ethan briefly swerved, but quickly straightened out the truck.

As he regained control, they both turned to look back at me as if I had grown a second head. I didn't know if it was because they were so focused on their conversation that they had forgotten I was even in the truck with them or what. Now they both looked at me like I had magically appeared and spoken those words from the back seat.

"Umm, Sasquatch, first of all, I did invite you," Ethan said quietly, using the same condescending tone with me as before. "I told you about that party in particular, just as I do with all the other parties and events that came up. In fact, if I recall correctly, I told you to bring Darlene. However, she did what she always did. She declined to join us because she thinks that we're beneath her. And so, since you do everything your woman says do, that's why you didn't go to the party. Which is also why you hadn't met Stacey up until just a few weeks ago. Second of all, shut the hell up!"

At this, Greg started chuckling. All I could do was sit back and let the truth of Ethan's words sink in.

I thought about how much I had missed out on because of the bad relationship that I was in. I was so glad things were over between me and Darlene.

"Finish what you were saying, man," Ethan said to Greg.

"Yeah, sure," Greg said. "Anyway, it was right after the fight ended and we both went outside to get some fresh air at the same time. I didn't say much to her after Stacey introduced us, but I was definitely checking her out. I mean damn! She's a fine ass woman!"

"Yessir, she sure is attractive," Ethan said, looking over at Greg and shaking his head approvingly and smacking his lips. "She has that plump, juicy booty and them big ole—"

"Hey, man!" Greg said, his left arm snapping out and jabbing Ethan hard on his arm.

"Ow! Damn! I was just messing with you, man," Ethan said, laughing as he rubbed his bicep.

"Whatever, man," Greg continued. "So anyway, we went outside and I turned on my suave charm, struck up a conversation with her and it was on from there. It was crazy! I didn't really think anything about it, but we just clicked. We were out there talking forever. Hell, you came looking for me because everyone was leaving but I was still outside talking, remember?"

"Yeah, I remember that. I didn't think anything about it," Ethan said. "I didn't know what y'all were doing out there."

"Dude," Greg said with a sad smile on his face. "We were out there talking about some of everything that night. We've been talking to each other just about every night since. We've definitely gotten closer over the past few months."

"Damn," Ethan said. "This must be serious, man. As long as we've known each other, I don't think I have ever heard you talk that way about any woman."

"Man, you don't even know," Greg agreed, slowly exhaling another deep sigh. "I thought I'd never have those feelings for another woman again until I met Angel. Anyway, I reached out to her week before last. I wanted to take that step with her. She's been asking me over and over for us to go out and really start dating. I've been hesitant in trying to do that, but I finally said to myself that it was time. I was tired of dealing with all the crap from the other chicks that I've been messing with. It was like each time I did my duty with them, the only thing I could think of was her. It's crazy, man."

"Damn," Ethan said again quietly.

"Yeah. Damn," Greg agreed. "I called her up to ask her out. My intent was to tell her that I wanted for us to really start going out as a couple, in the open, to let the world know that we're together. I wanted to take her out to the movies and to eat. At first she was happy as hell but the minute I said Red Lobster though, her whole mood changed. She starts saying that she wants to go to Pappadeaux instead."

"Pappadeaux? She wanted top notch, huh?" Ethan said.

"Top notch is right," he said. "But dude, the truth is that I don't have top notch money. I was going to do whatever it took to take her to where ever she wanted to go. Hell, I thought about going to holla at my boy D-Lo and do what I used to do in order to get some quick paper."

"You didn't call him, did you?" Ethan asked, snapping his head around to look at Greg. "Please tell me you didn't do that. I hope you didn't call him, man. You left that life a long time ago. Don't let no chick take you back there."

"No, man. I didn't," Greg said. "I said I almost called him. I'm not going to lie, I thought about it. I mean really thought about it. I can't go back to that, though. The last time I did, it ended up costing me three years of my life. I said the hell with that and I called her the next day. I told her straight up that I didn't have the money to take her to Pappadeaux . I told her that I'd have the money this week when I got paid and that I'd take her today. At first she agreed but then she calls me with some lame excuse about how she forgot that her and her girls were going out tonight.

"So, there I am," he continued, "hanging out with y'all fools and guess who shows up on the arm of some other dude?"

"I feel you," Ethan said.

Ethan looked like he was trying to find something to say in response to Greg's situation but instead just shook his head in silent understanding before reaching over to turn up the radio.

We each went silent, going into our own worlds as the truck rolled down the empty highway, listening as Marsha Ambrosius sang poignantly about a love that was so far away.

29

Ethan

*G*reg and I were making the trip to Ellenwood in relative silence after having dropped off Walter. I knew that Greg had a lot on his mind and wasn't in the mood for talking. I gave him his space and let the radio provide background noise for the ride over to his house.

"You going to be okay, man?" I asked Greg as I pulled in front of his house.

"Yeah, I'm cool," he responded as he opened the passenger door. "I just have a lot to think about. Everything that went down tonight made me realize that I want more than I thought I did. My mind is spinning right now. I'm going to go lay down and think things through."

"I feel you," I said as he got out of the truck and walked to his house.

I rolled down the window and called out to him. "It's going to work out, man. Hit me up tomorrow and we can run one."

Without looking back, Greg threw up a peace sign as he kept walking towards his front door.

Backing out of his driveway, I realized that I didn't want to go home to an empty house. The overwhelming ache of loneliness that I had become all too familiar with suddenly crept over me. I thought that I had gotten used to the feeling, become numb to the soft sadness of not having anyone special in my life.

I wasn't sure just what I wanted to do, but I knew that I didn't want to go home. I did not want to go back to my empty house. Not tonight.

I thought briefly about going to one of the many strip clubs throughout the city and supporting a few single moms. As much as I considered myself a true connoisseur and enjoyed watching the exquisite thickness of the best shoe models in the country gyrating and shaking all of the voluptuous assets that God had so abundantly blessed them with, tonight, I wasn't in the mood to do that.

A crazy thought crossed my mind and on an impulse, I decided to act on it. I checked the dash clock as I pulled to a stop at the entrance of Greg's subdivision, I picked up my cell phone and made the call.

"Hello, Sir," she said in that sexy voice that was beginning to take a hold of me with each word she spoke.

"Good morning," I said in response, a smile spreading across my face.

"It's not morning yet," Monica said. "We have a few more minutes to go. Getting an early start, aren't you?"

I felt instantly relieved when I heard the twinkle in her voice. I knew that I had made the right decision in calling her.

"I want to know why you're calling my phone at this crazy hour of the morning," she said. "I could be out on a hot date or something and you just call me all out the blue like this. That could've put me in an awkward position."

"Well, ma'am," I said, trying to use my most seductive voice. "If you were out on a hot date or something, then I know you wouldn't have answered the phone. I'd be talking to your voicemail right about now if that was the case, so let's not even go there. If you were out and you did choose to answer your phone, then that tells me that whoever you're with wasn't handling his business properly. Also, I'm sure that you've heard the old saying that after midnight, ain't but two things open: that's Waffle House and a pair of legs. According to this very accurate timepiece I'm wearing, it's now one minute after twelve. You know what that means, don't you?"

"Oh, really?" she said with a laugh. "You're an arrogant so-and-so, aren't you? Only two things open, huh? Please tell me what that means, Mr. Man. I really want to hear this one."

"It means that I'm hungry and I want to see you, so you need to leave whichever lame dude you're with that actually would let you be on the phone with another guy while you're out with him and meet me at Waffle House."

"You know what?" she said, laughing. "For your information, the only thing close to a dude around here is this stuffed teddy bear my son gave me for Mother's Day. I don't think Beary cares who I'm on the phone with. And as a matter of fact, I am a bit hungry, so

Waffle House sounds good. Which one, though? Lord knows there's one on every corner."

I laughed in agreement. "Yes, indeed. That's true. How about the one on Wesley Chapel Road? That's right in the middle from both of us."

"That's a good idea," she said. "I'll meet you there. Give me thirty minutes or so to get over there, okay?"

"Great! I'll see you then," I said, putting the truck in gear and pulling out of the subdivision.

As I drove out of Ellenwood and through DeKalb County heading towards Wesley Chapel road, I could not stop smiling. It seemed that ever since our evening out together, I was feeling Monica more and more. She had such a cool personality, great sense of humor, intelligence, business savvy—the whole package. I really wanted to know even more about her and I hoped that over time, I would be able to do just that.

I was on autopilot for the quick twenty minute ride as my mind replayed the events of the day, including the encounter between Angel and Greg. Before long, I was rolling down Wesley Chapel, crossing over I-20, and getting ready to make the turn into the Waffle House parking lot.

I slowly drove by her distinctively colored car in the sparsely filed lot and looked through the windows into the restaurant. I saw her sitting in a booth in the back gazing out into the parking lot. As our eyes met, we stared at each other for a long moment. She gave me a little finger wave along with her radiant smile. I played it cool and gave her a slight head nod in return.

I backed into a parking space next to her car and got out of my truck with a feeling of excitement and anticipation.

Entering the small diner, I was greeted with a mixture of sounds. A waitress was loudly calling out an order of scrambled eggs, hash browns scattered and covered, and bacon. The sharp metal clang of a spatula striking the iron surface of the grill reverberated in contrast to the smooth sounds of Grover Washington, Jr's, "Just the Two of Us" playing on the jukebox.

I walked over to the booth and sat down across from Monica who already had a cup of coffee sitting in front of her. Getting the waitress's attention, I indicated to her to bring me a cup as well.

"Well hell, Miss Lady," I said to Monica. "Thirty minutes, huh? It looks like you've been here for a while already. Here I was thinking I'd get here before you."

"Hey there, Mr. Man. Did you think I bought that car out there to drive Ms. Daisy around?" she said, pointing to the parking lot with her chin. "The SS doesn't stand for 'super slow'. I can make all four hundred and twenty-six horses gallop when I want them to."

"Nice!" I said, unable to hold back my grin and nodding my head in approval. "It's definitely good to see you again."

"Same here," she said, giving me a quick wink. "So what made you want to see me, anyway? And if you say anything about open legs, I'm going to walk right out."

I started smiling at this comment. *I needed this,* I thought as I looked into Monica's eyes.

"Well, I better not say what I'm thinking then," I said, wiggling my eyebrows up and down lasciviously as I added sugar and cream to the steaming cup of coffee that the waitress had just placed in front of me.

"Whatever, boy," she said, laughing. "And you still didn't answer my question."

"Have you ordered?" I asked, purposefully not answering her.

"No, not yet," she said. "I was waiting on you, so I just got some coffee."

"You can go ahead though," she said, picking up the laminated menu that was on the corner of the table. "I'm not exactly sure what I want so I'm going to need a few more minutes."

"I'll have an order of triple hash browns capped and chunked, please," I said to the waitress, indicating that I wanted ham and mushrooms added to my triple-sized order of hash browned potatoes.

"That's it for me, thanks," I said, returning my menu to its holder on the table.

"Damn, greedy," Monica said, shaking her head at me. "Are you going to leave some food for the rest of us?" Turning her attention to the waitress, she said, "I'll have the T-bone and eggs, please. Eggs scrambled with cheese, the steak cooked medium and a side of grits. Thank you."

"Hold up!" I said while giving the waitress a look of mock disbelief. "I'm greedy? She's ordering damn near a whole side of beef and I'm the greedy one?"

"I haven't eaten all day," Monica said, "What's your excuse?"

"I ate a little earlier when I was out with my boys," I replied. "That's really all I've eaten since I've been up since early this morning helping my man move his ex-girlfriend out of his spot and into her own apartment."

"That was nice of you to help," she said, nodding her head in approval.

"Yeah, I guess," I said wearily. "It's been a crazy day. I helped one of my boys with the end of his relationship and I found out my best friend has been having a secret one. That whole situation with him and the chick he thought he was with had to be the craziest thing I had ever seen."

"What do you mean that he thought he was with her?" she asked, giving me a confused expression.

I took another sip of my coffee and began to tell Monica about the events of my day. The smell of our food being prepared on the grill only a few feet from us filled the air. The mood in the diner was warm and relaxing and I was glad that I made the decision to meet her here. This was the perfect end to a long day.

30

Stacey

My ringing cell phone rudely interrupted me from the supreme comfort of deep, restful sleep. I didn't know what time it was, much less where I was, as I tried futilely to ignore the device's incessant ringing.

"Hullo," I mumbled groggily into the phone.

"Stacey? You up?" a female voice asked.

My brain was still foggy from sleep, so it took a few seconds for me to recognize it was Angel who had called and woken me up.

"Yes. I'm up, I'm up. What is it?" I muttered angrily, not even trying to fake politeness as I rolled over to turn on the lamp on the nightstand. I fumbled for the remote control that had fallen somewhere between the folds of my thick comforter. Finding it, I clicked off the television. I could not fall asleep without the white noise that it provided, but now that I was wide awake, the television was more of a distraction that anything else.

"I'm sorry to call this late and wake you," she said. "I know you're sleeping, but I had to talk to you," she said quickly, her words seeming to spill out of her.

"What's wrong, girl? Is everything okay?" my annoyance quickly being replaced with worry as I picked up on the anxiety in her voice.

"I'm okay, I guess," she replied. "Well, I'm okay physically. Emotionally, well, that's another story."

"I see," I said, the feeling of irritation creeping back into me. I looked over and saw the time displayed on my alarm clock. This woman always had some kind of issue going on, usually involving one man or another, and now she was calling me at damn near midnight with the latest installment of her drama.

I was her friend though. Part of that meant being there for her when she needed me, no matter what time that might be. I closed my eyes, slowly counted to ten, took a deep breath, and spoke slowly and calmly. "Angel, what's going on?"

She released a long sigh before she began to tell her story of confusion and heartbreak in words filled with so much pain. I was quiet, listening to her talk about Cory and how he seemed to be what she wanted on paper, but wasn't sure what was lying beneath the surface with him.

I listened in silence as she told me about how she ran into Ethan and his boys at the restaurant.

"His boys?" I interrupted. "Who was there with him?"

"It was him, Evan, Walter, and Greg. Why?" she asked.

"No reason. Just curious. Anyway, I'm sorry. What were you saying?" I said, pushing my rising anger at Walter back down. I was still ticked off with him and his fiancée.

I returned my attention to Angel who continued talking, telling me how she would have never in a million years thought that she could fall for someone like Greg. I heard all of the emotion in her voice as she recounted the events of the evening, and the pain that she felt as she looked at Greg and saw the hurt and betrayal on his face.

She fell silent as if all of her energy was spent. It was like she was drained from the experience of the evening now that she could finally let everything out.

"Wow! Greg?" I said stunned, not really knowing what to say. "So Greg's the mystery friend that you've been talking about all this time?" I asked, amazed at this revelation. "I never would have thought that you two would have anything in common, much less have a kinda-sorta relationship going on. Have you spoken to him since you saw him earlier?"

"No," she replied quietly. "I've wanted to call him so many times since Cory dropped me off, but I haven't. Each time I pick up the phone to call him, I can't bring myself to go through with it."

"Angel,' I said. "I never would've ever imagined that you would have a connection with Greg. But I do know that if he feels the same about you as you obviously feel about him, you need to make that call."

"I know, I know," she replied, "I will. I just can't. Not right now."

"Okay," I said, "Well, just know that I'm with you. I'll be here for you, no matter what."

"Thank you, Stacey," she said gratefully. "I'm so glad you answered the phone. I know I can be a handful at times, but knowing that you're always there for me…just knowing that you are my friend, I need that right about now. Thank you."

"Girl, don't mention it. I'm still mad at you for setting me up with that broke down Billy Dee Williams, but I'm still your friend," I said, trying to make her feel better and lighten the mood.

"I know, right? Thank you, girl," she said. "I need all the support I can get right about now."

"Well, I'm here. I have to ask though," I began carefully. "What about Cory?"

"What do you mean?" she asked, a trace of anxiety in her tone.

"Didn't he notice anything between you and Greg tonight?" I asked.

"No, I don't think so," she said. "Everything seemed to be fine the whole time that we were there at Quip. I mean, we hung out with them for over an hour and Cory seemed to be cool. On the ride home, we talked about the concert and made small talk. In fact," she added, her voice perking up, "he asked me out on another date."

"Really?" I asked, surprised to hear this. Most guys did not have the instincts that women did, but I was still surprised that Cory did not pick up on anything. Based on the way she had described the energy between her and Greg the entire evening that they were there together, I would have thought Cory might have detected something.

"So are you going out with him again?" I asked.

"Of course," she answered. "I don't know when though. I mean, he's a great guy and I really enjoyed myself toni…" She trailed off for a second before coming back on the phone. "Holy crap!" she said excitedly, "It's him calling me."

"Him who?" I asked. "Cory or Greg?"

"I gotta go. I'll call you tomorrow," she said quickly and clicked off before telling me who it was that was calling.

I held the now silent phone in my hand, recounting the details of the conversation. I said a prayer for my friend, hoping that she was making the right moves in her life. I knew that she was playing a potentially dangerous game by having both of these men pursuing her. I hoped she would handle the situation so that no one, including her would get hurt, but I knew that would be wishful thinking.

Sooner or later, she would have to make a choice between Greg and Cory. That could be a volatile situation for her to be in. The best scenario that I could envision would be her deciding on one man and telling the other that she could not see him any longer. She would then have to totally and completely end things with him before they got any deeper and more complicated.

Regardless of the decision she made, I knew that I would be there for her.

I put the phone on the night stand, turned on the television, clicked off the lamp, pulled the covers back over me, and tried to go back to sleep.

31

Angel

*A*fter quickly ending my call with Stacey, I put the phone
to my chest, closed my eyes, and tried to steady my nerves. My heart
had skipped a beat when I saw on the phone's display that it was
Greg calling. I didn't know what to expect from him.

I was well aware of his temper. I knew that when he got upset,
he got fire hot. I braced myself for the verbal onslaught that I was
sure would be coming.

"Why?" was the quiet question that he asked, getting right to the
heart of the matter.

I was caught off guard by this. The softness of his question
completely tore into me and I felt my heart breaking.

"I'm sorry, Greg," was all I could say as my eyes began to moisten.

His silence hit me with more force than any physical blow could
have possibly delivered.

The tears began to roll down my cheeks as I held the phone to my ear.

"I wasn't trying to hurt you," I continued, trying in vain to explain myself. "I'd already told Cory that I'd go out with him. That's the only reason that I told you I was going out with my girls tonight. I never in a million years thought you'd be in Quip or anywhere else we could have run into each other like we did. If I did, I promise you that we would have gone somewhere else."

The only sound over the phone connection was that of his car radio playing softly in the background.

"So what's the deal with y'all?" he asked. "Who is he?"

"We just work together," I said. "He's asked me out several times before. Tonight was the first time he and I have ever gone out on a date or even done anything outside of work-related functions since we met. You and I weren't even supposed to be going out tonight. We should've went out last weekend but you didn't have the mon—."

I tried to catch myself but it was too late. I regretted saying it the minute the word left my lips.

"I didn't mean it like that," I said, trying to recover the moment. "What I was trying to say was th—".

"Don't worry about it," he said with a chuckle, cutting me off. "I saw what time it was when ol' boy pulled out that platinum American Express card and waved it around. He made it a point that he would pay for everything tonight, even though we told him that we had it."

"No, Greg," I said, trying to defend Cory. "He was just trying to show his appreciation. If it wasn't for you guys letting us sit with y'all, we would probably still be waiting on a table to come open. He was just trying to be generous."

"If you say so," he said dismissively. "You can thank Ethan for that. Anyway, you're right. I don't have the money to take you out to all the places you want to go. I can't roll like your boy can. Not yet, anyway. Right now, I can only do what I can do. I know this much though, I have what it takes to handle you. I can take care of you. I can make you feel like no one else can. The question is, what do you really want?"

I had to think about this question. I did care about Greg. I cared about him a lot more than I ever thought I would, based on all the many differences between us.

Our physical relationship was incredible. It has always been, ever since the first time we got together sexually. The chemistry between us was unlike anything I had ever experienced with any man before him.

"I want us to be more than we are now, Greg," I said finally, knowing that this moment required me to be more honest with him than I had ever been. "But I don't think you can take care of me the way I want to be taken care of. That's what hurts me the most."

He again became quiet, allowing the silence to settle between us like a thick fog. The sounds of Chrisette Michele's, "Goodbye Game" coming from the stereo in his car in the background penetrated the emptiness.

"Greg? I have to know. What do you want?" I asked.

"You," he said, matter-of-factly, with no hesitation.

I closed my eyes, his simple yet powerful answer causing me to be at a loss for words.

"Where are you?" I asked, the realization clicking that he was obviously not at home.

"Not too far from you."

"What do you mean?" I asked in confusion.

I pulled the ends of my pink satin robe tight around my waist and quickly walked out of my kitchen. Going over to the bay window in the living room, I pulled the drapes aside to look out at the street in front of my house.

"Where are you?" I asked again, looking up and down the block, not seeing his car anywhere in sight.

"I'm in the parking lot of the Publix up the way from you," he said. "I was going to come over there earlier and go the hell off on you because I was so pissed. But I thought about it and realized that the only person that I should be mad at is myself."

"I know you're upset with me," I said. "I know I should've told you the truth about what I was doing tonight and who I would be doing it with. I just didn't want to hurt you."

"I probably could've dealt with that," he said. "I mean, you and I aren't really what I would call exclusive. But you didn't have to lie to me. I want us to at least be friends. Friends don't have to go through all that with each other."

I thought about this for a while. I knew he was completely right.

"So, is your boy Cory over there now?" he asked.

"Huh? Of course not," I said in surprise at his question. "There isn't anybody in this house except me. I'm here by myself."

"Good. I'll be there in a few minutes," he said and ended the call.

A short while later, I heard a knock at my door.

As soon as I opened it, Greg wordlessly pulled me into his arms. He lifted me off my feet and I automatically wrapped my legs around his thick torso and began kissing him like I had never done before.

We stood in the doorway passionately kissing for several minutes before he shuffled into the house with me still locked around his waist.

He kicked the door closed behind him and we slowly made our way over to the couch. When we ended up in my living room, I finally unlocked my legs from around him, enabling him to lower me to the floor.

He looked directly into my eyes as he wordlessly pulled off his shirt, undid his belt, unfastened his jeans, and kicked them off to the side by his feet.

As he stood there in only his white boxer briefs, my eyes trailed down his chest, down to the large print of his member stretching the cotton of his boxers.

Suddenly, quickly, he turned me around to face the couch. He then pulled my robe up above my hips, and slid my pink thong panties aside. Without any hesitation, he thrust himself deep inside me.

There was no resistance to his aggressive entrance because both my heart and my body were ready for him.

"OH! MY! GOD!" I screamed over and over again.

He was directly behind me as I lay bent over the armrest, my face buried in one of the cushions.

The forceful and rhythmical jackhammering of his thick manhood into me made me feel as if I were going to explode with the pleasure that was being pounded into me.

It would take more than the thick foam inside the cushion to muffle my screams and moans of ecstasy. It was all that I could take;

however, with each stroke, I wanted more and more, deeper and deeper, harder and faster.

My hands seemed to have minds of their own. I was frantically grasping out, trying to grab on to anything that was in reach—the edge of the couch, a pillow, my hair, just anything that I could hold onto to keep me steady as I travelled on this pleasure ride. I reached back, digging my nails into his thick thighs, trying my best to pull him even deeper into me.

"Take it! Take it!" I screamed, throwing my hips back towards him, meeting his powerful thrusts in a perfect rhythm that made my whole body shudder each time our midsections met. I was going crazy with the pleasure that was seemingly coursing through every vein in my body.

I felt his pace quicken, his grunts from the exertion of his labor of lust were getting louder. This turned me on even more as I was caught up in the total sensual magic of the moment. My body was so aroused that I could feel each drop of his sweat as it fell from him and softly sprinkled on the small of my bare back.

I was in total and complete ecstasy and felt myself coming closer and closer, riding the waves of pleasure that were propelled by his passion. Always in tune to my body, he felt my reactions and began to be more forceful, more aggressive, pushing himself deeper inside of me. He kept pounding me relentlessly, taking me closer to my explosion.

Finally, my dam was burst open by the force of his masculine onslaught. My body was rocking convulsively as my juices splashed all over his torso and ran down my thighs. I was overcome with involuntary spasms of me reaching my peak as Greg continued to relentlessly pound me.

I heard his guttural scream a few moments before I felt him exploding inside me. He twisted and bucked and pushed himself even deeper into me.

He then collapsed, the weight of his body feeling like a blanket on me. He hugged me close as the pain from his pleasure subsided.

As we both lay there attempting to catch our breath, I tried to figure out what had just happened. There was no denying that my body could not get enough of this man. No matter the time, day or night, I wanted him and I knew he felt the same for me. Sadly, however, I knew that once my heartbeat slowed and returned to a normal rate, reality would soon set in and things would be right where they left off.

32

Walter

With all of the emotional ups and downs today, from me moving Darlene into her apartment and out of my life, to riding in Ethan's truck while listening to Greg tell us about him and Angel, I was emotionally exhausted and ready to just go home and relax.

Go home. Those words had such a different weight to them now. I could not remember the last time that I actually wanted to go home. In fact, this was the first time today that I actually looked forward to going to my apartment.

I used the short walk from the parking lot where Ethan had just dropped me off to the front door of my apartment to reflect on just how much had changed in my life in the span of a few emotion-packed hours.

After moving Darlene into her new place earlier and then dropping off Ethan at his house, I finally got back to return the moving truck. Having been on the move all day, I now found myself with plenty of free time on my hands, but not really knowing what to do with it.

I decided to just sit in my car right there in the U-Haul service center parking lot and watch the people and cars coming and going on Covington Highway in Decatur. I clicked on the radio and listened to the last few minutes of the Georgia Bulldogs football game.

As the game ended with a win for the Dawgs, I sat in the reclined bucket seat, looking out the windshield. I watched the clouds lazily float by, thinking of what else I could do to kill some more time. I was enjoying the peace in that moment and did not really want to go back to my apartment. The truth was that I was looking for any reason to procrastinate.

It was hard to believe that for the past few weeks, I couldn't wait for Darlene to be gone. Now that she had moved out, I had to deal with the fact that I was going to be alone in the apartment. That was something I was honestly not looking forward to. I knew I would have to man up and deal with it. Later.

I finally decided to head over to the clinic and catch up on a few reports I needed to complete instead of going back to my apartment. I figured I had enough time to put in a few hours worth of work before heading home and getting ready to go out with the guys.

I let my seat up, fired up the engine, and listened to the throaty rumble of the Hemi engine as it idled. Putting the car in gear, I headed over to the clinic in Snellville.

I checked my watch as I pulled into the clinic's empty parking lot. I told myself that I would spend no more than one hour working.

That should give me enough time to get home and figure out what I would wear out tonight.

It was well into the third hour of me being there as I had completely lost track of time. It was a good thing that Ethan called to tell me that he would be over to pick me up in an hour or else I probably would still have been there.

Quickly locking up the office, I rushed over to my apartment. I ran inside and went straight to my bedroom closet before rushing into the bathroom.

I barely had enough time to take a shower and get dressed, and didn't even look around the apartment while I was there. I was brushing my teeth right as Ethan called to tell me that they were outside.

Now, only six hours later as I walked to the front door, the sound of Ethan's truck fading away as he pulled out of my quiet apartment complex. I now had time to think about things. I put the key in the lock, closed my eyes for a few seconds as I held the knob in my hand. Finally, I twisted it, opened the door, and walked inside to face my new reality.

I stood in the middle of my living room in my apartment, stunned as I looked around at all of the empty space. The only things left were my old recliner which I have had for about the last four years and my flat screen television, once mounted on an elegant floor stand, but was now propped against a far wall.

"Damn, she took everything!" I said in exasperation as I surveyed the living room. I had not really taken a true inventory as to how empty the apartment really was until just this moment.

The indentations in the carpet where the couch and coffee table once stood were the only proof that there had even been any furniture in the room to begin with. The walls, which once held artwork and photos were now bare. As I walked through each of the empty rooms, I became depressed as to just how little I had to show for not only all of the years with Darlene, but for my life in general.

She had moved in and slowly, I had moved out. It amazed me to think that we lived together and this apartment should have been ours, but as I looked at the large amount of nothing now surrounding me, I realized that everything was hers.

I walked through the living room towards the kitchen, shaking my head at how my footsteps were echoing throughout the empty space. I made mental notes of everything I would need to purchase over the next few weeks, wondering if I should buy them now or wait until after I closed on my new house.

I decided to get a snack while I figured out my next move. I knew there was a bottle of orange soda in the fridge. I pulled the door open and was shocked that not only was the soda gone, but there was absolutely nothing else in there. Even the box of Arm & Hammer Baking Soda which was usually all the way in the back was gone.

I opened the freezer door and saw that it was empty as well. All of the beef, chicken, ice cream, and other frozen foods were gone. Even the ice cube maker was empty. The canister that stored the ice had been dumped out and was sitting empty on the middle shelf. I shook my head in disbelief when I noticed the switch that ran the device was in the off position.

Closing the freezer, I went to the pantry to see if it was empty as well. Sure enough, all of the shelves were bare. The canned goods, breakfast cereal, and everything else that used to be stored there were gone.

I stepped back in amazement. I couldn't believe it.

I knew that she hadn't taken it with her because I didn't remember taking any boxes containing food into her apartment when we were moving her in. Darlene must have gone back inside when we were loading the truck and thrown everything in the fridge away. I crossed my fingers hoping that I was wrong and maybe there was another explanation. A quick check inside the trash can confirmed without a doubt that she had in fact dumped all of the food.

I shook my head in disgust as I saw packages of ground turkey, yogurt, and even worse, the bag of chips that I had been looking forward to snacking on. She had taken the time to empty the contents of the ketchup, milk, and orange juice bottles into the trash bag as well.

I slammed the lid closed and walked back into the living room seething at how spiteful it was of her to do this. Darlene was supposed to be out of my life, but as usual, she managed to disrupt everything around me.

I've got to get out of this house, I thought as I grabbed my car keys.

There was a Quiktrip convenience store not too far from my apartment, so I figured I'd go there and grab a couple of hot dogs. I knew they weren't the healthiest things to be eating this late, but I wasn't really that sleepy and seeing all of my food dumped in the trash really perturbed me.

I could not believe she could be that petty. I know she was upset with how things went down, but this was too much. I was getting more irritated the more I thought about how tonight summed up my entire relationship with her.

Pulling out of my apartment complex, I picked up my cell phone and called her. The phone rang with no answer. I knew she wouldn't answer. I knew she was up but didn't want to take my call. Right before the voice mail began, I ended the call.

After waiting a few seconds, I punched the SEND button to call her again. This time I let the call go through to voice mail.

I listened to her recorded voice on the voice mail greeting before ending the call again without leaving a message. I held the phone in my hand as I drove down the empty road, thinking about why I had even called her in the first place. What was the point? She was out of my life and no matter what she did or didn't do, the bottom line was she was gone. Yes, she found a way to thumb her nose at me on her way out the door, but right about now, it didn't even matter.

I was smiling to myself as a peace settled over me. The realization hit that I would not have to deal with Darlene any longer. Not only that, I was pulling into the parking lot of Club Quiktrip, the nickname for the Panola Road Quiktrip store. No matter what time of day or night, the huge convenience store was always busy. On any given Saturday night, the parking lot would be filled with people, both in the store itself or outside at the gas pumps. This store was truly a beehive of people coming and going so there was usually at least one DeKalb County police officer parked in their squad car in front of the store just in case things got a little too wild.

I managed to find a parking space on the back side of the building and headed in. I went straight to the hotdog stand, made myself two hotdogs loaded with relish, ketchup, and mustard. On my way to the cashier stand, I grabbed a bag of Doritos from the rack. The store was bubbling with energy as all the people were engaged in animated conversations with each other. This was truly a welcome distraction from my quiet apartment and also Darlene and her foolishness.

It was finally my turn at the cashier. I paid for my items, left the store, and got into my car. Sitting there in the parking lot, I opened the chips and watched the different people entering and leaving the store.

One couple in particular held my attention. She was an attractive woman and he was an equally handsome man. I watched as he held both the inner and outer doors open for her to enter. The look of love and appreciation that she gave him was breathtaking to witness. He lovingly placed his hand on her back and guided her inside.

They eventually disappeared from my view, however the affection that they exhibited stayed with me. I wanted that. I deserved that. Now that Darlene was gone, I could finally have that.

As I backed out of my parking space, a silver car zipped right behind my bumper, barely missing hitting me. The car didn't even slow down as it sped out of the parking lot.

Damn! That was close, I thought as I watched its tail lights quickly disappeared down the road.

After that close call, I made sure to check both ways before slowly backing out. Safely out of the parking lot, I picked up my phone, scrolled through my address book, and called her.

33

Stacey

For the second time tonight, my phone began ringing. I punched my pillow in frustration as I reached over and picked it up. Fumbling with it as I tried to answer, I groused to myself, *I guess it wasn't meant for me to get any sleep tonight.*

Thinking that it was Angel calling me back, I didn't bother looking at the caller ID display before answering.

"Hey, girl," I said, "I wasn't expecting you to call back tonight. The way you got off the phone earlier, I didn't think I would hear from you until later on."

"Hello, Stacey," a male voice said.

I sat up in surprise. Quickly pulling the phone down from my ear, I now checked the caller ID to see who was calling. I was shocked to see Walter's name on the display.

"Stacey? You there? It's me, Walter," he was saying as I brought the phone back up to my ear.

"Yes, I'm here. Hello," I answered. "Sorry about that. I thought you were Angel."

"No, it's just me," he said with a nervous laugh. "Sorry for calling you so late. I just had to talk to you."

"Is everything okay?" I asked, wondering if he was in some kind of trouble. The way this night was turning out, I wouldn't be surprised.

"Yes, everything's fine," he said. "Like I said, I just had to call you because…well, because I made a serious step in my life today. I called you earlier to tell you but I got your voicemail."

"Yes, I saw that you called," I said, thinking back to earlier in the day. When I saw him calling, I looked at the phone and didn't bother to answer. I was still angry with him and his fiancée. Now, he had gotten lucky with his unexpected call. Since he was able to get through my defenses, I would give him the opportunity to say what he had to say. After that, I was going to blast with both barrels and let him have it for not telling me that he was engaged to be married and for leading me on.

"So, what were you calling for? What's going on?" I asked coldly.

"Well, I was calling you then for the same reason I'm calling you now," he said. "Ever since we met, I've been struck by you. Your style, your beauty, your intelligence, your sexiness, everything. I know we've only had a few phone calls here and there, but with each conversation, I've become more and more taken with you."

"Struck by me, huh?" I asked, trying to keep the smile out of my voice. I was trying to maintain my edge with him, but he completely caught me off guard with his sweet words.

"Yes. Very," he said. "I know this is all very sudden, but I want to get to know you even better. To do that, I want to put everything out in the open. I moved my ex-girlfriend out of my apartment today. I know I've only briefly mentioned her to you but you know I haven't been happy in a long time. It wasn't until I met you that it hit home just how much I was really missing."

I closed my eyes and lay back on my pillow. Hearing him say those words stirred something in me that I thought no one would ever be able to reach again. I felt something as well when we met but I thought it would pass and things would go back to normal.

I flashed back to my lunch encounter with Darlene. She said Walter was her fiancé, however listening to him, he said that she was only his girlfriend. Which was it? Someone wasn't telling me the truth and before I could move forward, I had to find out.

"Walter, I have to ask and please be honest," I said, knowing that the only way to get a straight answer was to ask a straight question. "Were you and Darlene engaged?"

"Engaged?" he said in surprise. "Hell no! We've been dating, if you want to call it that. I've never asked her to marry me though. Never. Why do you ask?"

"Just something someone told me. Never mind," I said, trying to put everything together.

"Oh, okay," he said. "Nah. We're, or should I say, we were far from being engaged. I'd love to take that step with someone one day.

The right someone, though, and that definitely wasn't Darlene. After the night I had tonight, I knew I'd made the right decision with her. She is truly the wrong person for me. After tonight with my boys and seeing just how unpredictable life can be, I knew I had to call you and tell you exactly what I was feeling."

"Yes, I heard all about your evening," I said, laughing, feeling my defenses falling, my spirits rising. "It sounded like an episode of some silly daytime soap opera."

"It felt like one too," he agreed. "I'm glad that it's over though, I can tell you that much. In fact, I'm on my way back home now."

"Back home?" I asked, "You're just now heading home? You didn't get enough excitement and had to go out for more?"

"I've had enough drama these last few days to last a lifetime," he said, chuckling. "I'm ready for some peace and quiet. I'm actually heading back home from Quiktrip."

"Oh, okay," I said. "Which QT did you go to?"

"Panola Road," he said. "It's right up the way from my apartment. I came home earlier but had to get out the house. I had a lot on my mind and didn't want to be alone in my empty apartment."

"You won't be living there much longer though," I said. "You'll be moving into your new townhouse in no time. I'm sure that you should be hearing back from the bank pretty soon. We'll have a closing date before you know it."

"I can't wait," he said.

"You made it home already?" I asked as I heard keys jingling and then a door opening. I could tell that he had switched on the speakerphone feature on his phone because all of the background noise suddenly got louder.

"Yep," he said, "Just walked in the door. I'm not sleepy so I'm proba—" He abruptly stopped talking and there was silence for a few seconds.

"Walter? What's wrong?" I asked, sitting up in the bed wondering what had happened to him.

"What are you doing here?" I heard him saying.

"Hello, baby," a woman's voice said. "I'm so glad you made it home, Sweetheart. I've been missing you."

"Darlene, what the hell are you doing here?" he asked again.

"I live here, silly," she said, giggling. "I know you really don't want me to leave. We both know you wanted me to stay, so I came back home to be with you."

"Back up off of me, Darlene!" he snapped. "Don't touch me. This is crazy, man! You got to go! I've told you I don't know how many times. We're through! Look, I don't want to be with you. You've got to leave. Now!"

"Oh, Walter, you don't mean that, baby," she cooed. "You're just tired from watching me pretend to leave you today. I'm sure that real estate bitch, Stacey or whatever the hell her name is, has you confused about what you and I have together. Don't worry though. When I met her the other day, I told her in no uncertain terms that she needs to leave my future husband alone and stay out of our lives. It's okay, baby. She won't be a problem anymore."

My heart stopped when she brought up our meeting. I knew something was off with her after our encounter in the restaurant but I couldn't put my finger on it. Listening to her now though, I knew for a fact that she was certifiable.

"Wait a minute. You met her?" he boomed. "Future husband? So that's why she asked if I was engaged," he said in a quieter tone, as if he was talking to himself. "Why would you do that? What's wrong with you?"

"Nothing's wrong with me, Walter," she said angrily. "Why does everyone keep asking me that? I love you. You love me. That's all there is to it. I let you go through with the game of moving me today but I know that you were only testing me. And see, here I am. I'm here for you. I'm the only person for you, Walter."

I could not believe what I was hearing. I've heard about psycho women but hearing one utter the words that Darlene was saying made my skin crawl. I prayed that Walter would be careful and get her out of there soon.

"Darlene," Walter said firmly. "I'm not going to say it again. Get the hell out of here."

"I'm not going anywhere," Darlene said angrily. Her voice took on a harsher, more sinister quality. "And neither are you. We're going to be together. The way it's supposed to be."

"Look, Darlene," Walter said, "I don't know wha—what the hell! Put the gun down!"

My blood ran cold at hearing that. *A gun? Oh, my God!*

"No, Walter!" Darlene screamed shrilly. "You're just like all of the others. You say you love me. You say you want to be with me, but then you kick me aside and run off with somebody else. I won't let that happen to me again. I love you and you love me and we're going to stay together!"

"What others? What are you talking about? Please put the gun down, Darlene," Walter said in a soothing, quiet tone, trying to defuse the situation. "Please, give me the gun and we can talk, okay?"

"No! You want to hurt me just like the rest of them," she shrieked.

"Darlene, please give me the gun," Walter said, his voice a soft plea. "I don't want to hurt you, I promise. Please give me the gun and we can talk, okay? Just hand it to me. Please give me the gun. Please."

"Stay back!" she screamed, her voice shrill filled with anger. "Stay away from me! I won't let you hurt me!"

POP!

POP!

POP!

The loud gunshots thundered through the phone causing me to drop it in surprise.

"Walter! Walter" I yelled hysterically into the phone as I quickly picked it up off the bed.

There was no response. The only sounds coming over the connection were Walter's moans of pain.

"I'm sorry, baby," Darlene said as she cried, her sobs getting louder. "Why'd you make me have to do that to you?"

I could not believe this was happening. I knew that I had to do something but I just didn't know what to do.

I got out of my bed and ran into Brianna's room and woke her up, the whole while I kept my phone pressed to my ear. The only thing I heard over the line were Darlene's sobs mixing grimly with Walters moans.

"Brianna! Get up," I said frantically. "Where's your phone?"

She barely cracked open her eyes as she wordlessly reached under her pillow and produced her phone.

"It's 0 1 2 0," she mumbled before rolling over, pulling the covers up over her head, and going back to sleep.

It took me a second to understand what she was saying before it clicked. With my phone still to my ear, I took hers and punched in the code to unlock it. Pulling up the keypad, I searched the address book for Ethan's number and hit SEND.

34

Ethan

*R*ubbing my hands together in eager anticipation, I couldn't wait to dive into my food as I watched our waitress bring the plates to our table. She was balancing two plates on her left arm while holding a third in her right, all while a bottle of warm waffle syrup dangled off her pinky finger.

"And here are your hash browns, capped and chunked," she said as she put the last plate in front of me. She placed Monica's food in front of her, including a thick T-Bone that was so large that covered every inch of the plate it sat on.

"I believe that's everything. Do you need anything else? Some more coffee?" she asked.

"No, thank you. We should be okay," I said, looking at Monica who nodded in agreement.

I took Monica's hand across the table and blessed our food.

When I finished, I eyed her juicy steak and said, "That looks pretty good. You're going to share that with me, right?"

"Nope," she said, looking directly at me as she cut off a huge chunk of meat. She slowly waved her fork in front of my face a few times before putting it in her mouth and chomping down.

"Mmmmmm," she said, smacking her lips dramatically. "This is soooo good!"

"Oh, you wrong for that," I said, laughing as I sprinkled salt and pepper on my hash browns.

I had just put a heaping forkful of the mound of steaming hot potatoes into my mouth when my phone started ringing.

"You've got to be kidding," I groaned, rolling my eyes at the interruption as I pulled the phone out of my pocket.

The display indicated that it was Brianna calling. I knew she wouldn't be calling me at this hour so it had to be Stacey borrowing her phone.

I quickly swallowed my food before answering, "Whattup? I guess you heard, huh?" I said in greeting, thinking she must have spoken to Angel and was calling me to talk about them.

"Ethan! Walter's been shot," Stacey screamed.

My smile instantly disappeared as my brain struggled to comprehend Stacey's words. I prayed I had not heard her correctly and that it was just a bad joke.

"Shot?" I asked in disbelief.

Monica, who had been slathering strawberry jelly on her toast, snapped her head up and looked at me in surprise. She put the food down and reached over and placed her hand on top of mine and gave it a reassuring squeeze.

"What's going on?" she mouthed, her face filled with concern.

I looked into her compassionate eyes and shrugged my shoulders helplessly in response to her question. I was glad she was with me because I wasn't sure how I would have handled this shocking news if I was alone. Once again, I was so happy I had made the decision to call her and even more grateful she accepted my invitation to join me.

"What happened?" I asked Stacey, returning my attention to the phone. "Take a deep breath, calm down, and tell me everything. Where is he? Who shot him?"

Stacey began telling me of her earlier conversation with Walter and how Darlene had gone back to his apartment and was there waiting for him.

"I can't believe she shot him! What's wrong with her?" she asked breathlessly, still in a state of shock.

"It sounds like she snapped," I said, trying to come up with some kind of an explanation as to what caused Darlene's inexplicable actions.

"You need to try and keep it together, Stace," I said soothingly. I didn't want her to get even more upset than she was now. I could only imagine how helpless she felt listening to everything going down and not being able to do anything about it.

"When did all of this happen?" I asked.

I had dropped Walter off less than an hour ago and he was fine then. I didn't stick around long because I had to drop off Greg.

Was Darlene already there waiting for him when I dropped him off? I wondered as I recalled the last image I had of him getting out the truck, dapping us up, and then walking into his apartment.

"Not even five minutes ago," she said. "That's why I'm calling you from Brianna's phone. I'm still listening to Walter yelling in pain on my phone now. Oh my God, Ethan! He's dying!"

"It just happened?" I asked in confusion. "Wait a minute. Have you called the police?"

"No, I haven't," she said, getting even more upset. "You were the first person that came to mind when I heard the gunsh—"

She abruptly went silent. I could tell she was still there by her rushed breathing over the phone connection.

"Stacey? Stacey? What's going on?" I asked anxiously.

"This is Stacey, that's who," I heard her saying. "I heard everything. I can't believe you would do that to him. You say you love him but then you shoot him?"

"What are you talki—" I began, confused as to what she was talking about. Then it hit me that she had to be talking to Darlene on the other phone.

"It doesn't matter now," she said. "You shot him. Do you really think he's going to want to be with a woman that shot him? What the hell's wrong with you?"

She paused for a few seconds before speaking again.

"Whatever, Darlene. The police will be there in a few minutes to arrest your crazy ass. You can save all of that nonsense for them. And you better believe I'm going to tell them everything I heard."

"Hello? Hello?" Stacey said before returning to the call with me. "That crazy broad hung up, Ethan," she said angrily. "I just remembered why I called you first. I was going to call the police but I realized that I don't know his address. I have his information back at the office, but not here at home with me. Please tell me that you have it so I can call the cops and an ambulance so they can go and help him."

"Hold on," I said as I started scrolling through the contact list in my phone until I came to Walter's name. I gave Stacey the address before telling her, "I'm a few minutes away from his apartment. I'm going to head over there right now. I'll call you as soon as I get there. Keep your phone close, okay?"

"Okay. I will," Stacey said. "Be careful, okay?"

"No doubt," I said as I ended the call.

Standing to my feet, I pulled out my wallet and took out two twenty dollar bills to take care of the bill.

"I hate to cut out early, but I've got to go," I said as I left the money on the table and turned to head towards the door. "Walter's apartment is the next exit up from here and I need to go and check on my boy. I'll call you tomorrow and fill you in on everything then, okay?"

"Anyway. So, are we taking your car or mine?" Monica asked, gathering up her purse and getting to her feet to stand beside me.

I stopped and looked at her.

"Huh?" I asked in disbelief. "You're coming with me?"

"Of course," she said, taking my hand in hers. "I'm here, Ethan. I'm with you. I'm not going to let you go running off by yourself in a time like this."

I was shocked. For so long, I'd wanted a woman who would ride with me, no questions asked, no matter what the situation was.

Finally, here was that kind of woman standing right here with me. All of this time, I had her number and I could kick myself for not calling her sooner.

I looked down into her eyes and squeezed her hand gently.

"Thank you," I said quietly and pulled her in close to me and gave her a quick kiss. That brief moment allowed me to calm down, relax, and focus on the situation at hand.

"We'll take my truck," I said as we made our way out of the restaurant and to the parking lot.

Holding the door of the truck open for her, I said, "I'm not sure when we'll be able to come back and get your car, but I'll work it out."

"That's cool," she said as she climbed in.

As we pulled out of the parking lot, I wondered to myself if this day could possibly get any crazier. I shook that thought out of my mind because I knew you should never tempt fate. If things could get any worse, they usually did.

On the short drive over to Walter's apartment, I filled Monica in on my conversation with Stacey and gave her the full story of Walter and Darlene. I told her about how they had met several years ago and had developed their strange, loveless relationship. I filled her in on how domineering Darlene was and how docile Walter had become in comparison since they had been together. I explained how they had finally broken up and Walter subsequently kicking her out of his apartment.

Monica listened quietly as I described how Walter and Stacey had met and the instant attraction they had to each other. She nodded in understanding when I told her how Stacey had given Walter the clarity that he needed to make the dramatic changes in his life that he had recently made. She occasionally asked me questions about Darlene. As I tried to find the answers to her questions, I realized how little I knew about Darlene.

The truck's big V-8 engine was roaring as we had made the trip on I-20 from Wesley Chapel to Panola Road in only a few minutes. Taking the exit on to Panola, we were quickly racing towards Walter's apartment.

Just as we were pulling up to the intersection in front of the Quiktrip convenience store, we were surprised as a silver car came careening through the intersection ahead of us, running the red light.

In that split second, I realized that the silver blur that had shot into the intersection was Darlene's Lexus. I knew it was hers by the reflective silver personalized license plate on the front bumper.

"That's Darlene!" I yelled. As we got closer, her features becoming more defined and I could make her out sitting behind the wheel.

At the same instant her car crossed into the middle of Panola Road, an eighteen-wheeler which was rumbling along slammed into Darlene's car in a loud, explosive crash, practically slicing off the entire rear end of the vehicle. The force of the impact caused the car to go into a violent, clockwise spin, eventually ending up in twisted heap in the parking lot of the Checker's restaurant that was on the corner.

It might have only taken a few seconds at most for the whole surreal episode to unfold, but the collision looked like it was a thirty second slow motion action scene from a Hollywood movie.

I slammed on the brakes and brought my truck to a screeching, sliding stop.

Snatching off my seat belt, I jumped out and ran over to the mangled remains of Darlene's car.

There was steam hissing from the radiator caused by the car having plowed into one of the concrete trash cans that were by the curb in front of the restaurant. The sound of the horn blaring was deafening as I got closer to the car.

"Darlene? Darlene?" I yelled repeatedly, hoping that she would respond.

I ran around to the driver's side door and looked inside the car. I didn't know if she was alone or if she had done something crazy like kidnapping Walter. As deranged as she had been tonight, I wouldn't put anything past her. I looked on the back seat, half expecting to see Walter tied up and bleeding. I breathed a sigh of relief when I saw that it was empty.

Through the cloud of smoke created by the discharged airbags, I could make out Darlene's limp body slumped over the steering wheel. Her face was a bloody mass of skin and hair, and I could only pray that she was still alive. As much as I despised her and knew that she was obviously a sick woman who desperately needed to get mental help, I didn't want to see her die.

"Darlene!" I yelled again as I tried in vain to wrench her door open.

It would not budge. The metal was so tangled that the door was twisted rendering it unopenable. It would take the Jaws of Life to get any of the doors open in order to get her out. I could hear the sirens of what I hoped was an ambulance approaching in the distance. I prayed that Darlene would hold on long enough to make it until they could get to the scene.

"Darlene! Can you hear me?" I yelled.

I quickly took off my shirt and wrapped it around my forearm and elbow. With a quick, powerful thrust, I drove my elbow through the window causing it to shatter into tiny pebbles. The small chards of glass flew into the passenger space and several pieces struck Darlene in the face.

With the glass broken, the acrid, smoky cloud inside began to clear out as fresh air rushed into the car. Darlene began to cough weakly as it was now easier for her to breathe.

"Ohhhhh," she groaned as she slowly raised her head a few inches off the steering wheel.

She stared at me through glassy eyes for a long while, her moans becoming weaker, her breathing becoming more difficult.

"Tell...him," she said weakly through clenched teeth as the pain enveloped her body.

"Tell...him...that...I...love...him," she said, her breathing labored as she struggled to say each word. She smiled weakly at me, closed her eyes, and slumped against the steering wheel.

"No! Darlene!" I yelled frantically shaking her, but it was no use. She was gone.

35

Angel

My head was nestled in Greg's lap where I lay curled on the couch with him. He was sitting in his underwear, his feet kicked up on the coffee table as he watched football highlights on ESPN.

My phone began ringing across the room and I almost let it ring through to voicemail. Instead, I got up and went into the kitchen to answer it and was glad I did. I held the phone to my ear and listened as Stacey told me about what had happened to Walter. I could only listen in amazement as she recalled the events that led up to him getting shot.

Never in a million years would I think Darlene would react the way she did and ultimately end up shooting him. I was shocked that she would do something like that. There were so many questions to be answered as this crazy drama unfolded. That was the kind of thing that you hear about when it was being reported on the news. I never imagined it could happen this close to me, to people that I knew.

I didn't know either Walter or Darlene all that well as I'd only interacted with them on one occasion. I met them a few years ago at a party that Ethan had thrown to celebrate the purchase of his tenth truck. Walter was an engaging guy one-on-one, but it seemed as if his entire demeanor changed whenever Darlene was around him.

She was a strikingly pretty woman but the way she spoke to him. I could not believe that she had any love or respect for him. She seemed to want to have total control over him, and for some reason, he allowed this to happen.

He struck me as a good guy but was weak when it came to dealing with his woman. I had run across guys like Walter before and they were not appealing at all to me. For some reason though, Stacey was attracted to him and listening to her almost hysterical account of his getting shot made my heart break for her.

I was walking back into the living room just as Greg answered his phone. "Whattup?' he said gruffly, picking up the remote to turn down the volume of the television.

He was quiet for a few minutes as he listened to whatever the person on the line had to say, his face not revealing anything.

"Okay, I'll be there in a few minutes," he said as he ended the call.

"Is everyting okay?" I asked.

"Yeah. If it's not one thing, it's something else," he muttered as he rubbed his face with his palms.

"Why?" I asked, wondering what else had happened. "What happened? Who was that?"

"That was Ethan. Darlene just died in a car accident," he said matter-of-factly, getting off the couch and gathering his clothes.

"What?" I said in surprise, my hand shooting up to cover my mouth. "What happened? I was just coming to tell you that I had to go to the hospital to meet Stacey. Darlene shot Walter and he's in intensive care. And now she's dead?"

Greg stepped into his pants and zipped them, at the same time relaying the information that Ethan had just given him. He told me that right after shooting Walter, Darlene had run a red light and was hit by an eighteen-wheeler. The worst part of his story, if that was even possible, was when he said she died right in front of Ethan, who was trying to get her out of the wrecked car.

"Oh my God!" I gasped. "He watched her die?"

"Yep, he was right there," Greg replied with a deep sigh. "He said that she closed her eyes and took her last breath."

I listened as he spoke, my mind trying to take it all in. I could not believe this night was happening. It was like ten of my worst bad dreams rolled into one epic nightmare.

I felt a wave of exhaustion sweep over me, and all I could do was sit down heavily on the couch.

"You okay?" Greg said, coming over and sitting next to me, putting his arm around my shoulder.

"Yes, I think so," I said wearily, leaning my head against his chest. "It's just been one hell of a night, that's all. First me and you and now all this."

"I feel you," he said as he took my hand in his. "I don't want to leave but I've got to meet Ethan and Stacey at the hospital. I'll call you when I get there, okay?"

"Do you mind if I go with you?" I asked, turning to look up at him.

"Are you sure?" he asked hesitantly.

"Yes. Since you're going there anyway, I can comfort Stacey," I said, thinking back to how she sounded when she called earlier. I also didn't want to be alone. I would much rather be with Greg, Stacey and Ethan instead of being in my bed alone, tossing and turning.

"Okay, cool," he said as he got up to put on his shoes. "Go throw on some clothes. I'll be in the car."

I quickly put on some jeans and a T-shirt, locked up the house, and went to the car. I smiled as Greg got out and walked around the car to hold the door open for me. Once seated inside, my smile quickly faded.

The ride to the hospital was a tough one because no matter how hard I tried, I could not get comfortable. As much as I would have loved to blame it on the extraordinary circumstances of the day, the truth was that Greg's car was the source of my discomfort.

With its torn seats, gaping holes in the carpeting covering the floorboards under my feet, and cracked windshield, his car was just plain ugly. To make matters worse, its slipping transmission that caused the whole car to jerk painfully as it changed gears, was both uncomfortable to ride in and embarrassing to be seen in.

My mind flashed back to the plush interior of Cory's car and how good it felt to be seated in the soft leather seats. I could not help but compare the two cars as I surveyed the interior of Greg's Honda Accord that had to be at least fifteen years old.

I thought about the two men and how the cars that they drove illustrated their many differences. Greg really and truly didn't care about such things as fancy new cars. He once told me that as long as his car got him from Point-A to Point-B safely and reliably, then he was satisfied. He was not opposed to getting a newer car, but it was not that high on his list of priorities.

Cory on the other hand made sure to surround himself with only the best that money could buy. From his car to his wardrobe, he always looked like success and wanted to make sure that everyone knew it.

I thought I knew what I wanted and I really believed the feelings I was having for Greg were real. I knew he overwhelmingly met all of my emotional needs. I knew from the exquisite soreness between my thighs that he satisfied all of my physical wants and then some.

Cory satisfied my desire to be with a man that could provide all my financial desires. I didn't want to think of myself as a gold-digger; however, I did know that I didn't want to be with a man who was comfortable with driving an old car and living in a rented house. I knew that Cory had his demons. He could even be a bit controlling at times as he had exhibited earlier, but I'm sure it wasn't anything that could not be overcome.

I shook my head, trying to clear my mind. *Why was I thinking about these things at a time like this?* I thought as I laid my head back against the headrest.

I should be supporting my friends instead of worrying about Greg and Cory and comparing them to each other. People were dying and getting shot and I was thinking about the comfort of the cars that they drove.

I bet Cory had 1500 count, Egyptian cotton sheets that were so soft and luxurious, they felt like you were sleeping in baby oil, I thought as my mind began to wander again.

What's wrong with me? I thought as I vigorously shook my head back and forth in an effort to get my rambling thoughts under control. Why was I always so consumed with material things?

I was trying to find the answers to these questions just as we pulled up to the emergency room of the DeKalb Medical Center at Hillandale. There were several police cars and an ambulance parked by the entrance, their red and blue lights strobing, making the area light up like a night club dance floor.

Greg slowly drove through the parking lot until he found a parking space and backed in. He parked the car and got out of the driver's seat while I gathered my purse.

Just as I was getting ready to open my door, I was startled when it seemingly opened on its own. I looked up in surprise at Greg standing there holding the door open, waiting on me to get out the car.

Now that is something I could get used to, I thought.

I suppressed a smile as I got out and quietly said, "Thank you."

As we walked to the hospital's entrance, Greg pointed out Ethan's truck parked a few feet away from Greg's car.

"He told me they'd be sitting in the waiting room," he said as we walk inside the hospital's entrance.

There were about ten people seated in various places in the small waiting room. Everyone was either engaged in quiet conversation, reading magazines, napping, or playing with their smartphones, all waiting on news about their loved ones.

I saw Ethan sitting between Stacy and another woman in a row of chairs positioned against the back wall of the room.

The space had a sad air about it, but both women had smiles on their faces. The source of their smiles was probably from whatever Ethan was saying to them judging from the way he was wildly waving his arms around in front of him.

"Whattup, y'all," Greg boomed, his voice cutting through the relatively quiet space causing everyone in the waiting room to turn and look at us.

"Whattup, dude. Damn you loud as hell," Ethan said as he stood up to greet us.

"Whatever," Greg said, reaching out and giving him a brotherly hug. "I told you a thousand times that I learned how to whisper in a helicopter."

"Aint that the damn truth," Ethan said with a chuckle.

"Hey, Angel," he said, moving over and leaning down to give me a hug. "Good to see you with my boy here."

"Whatever, Ethan," I said as I returned his hug. "You're worrying about the wrong thing."

"Let me go check on my friend," I said, stepping around the two men and going over to Stacey.

"Hey, girl," I said, giving her a tight hug. As I held her, I could feel all of the tension in her body.

"It's going to be okay," I whispered as I rubbed her back.

The woman that had been seated next to Ethan stood by quietly, not seemingly not wanting to interrupt our moment.

I stepped back from Stacey to introduce myself. I wasn't sure who she was or what relation she was to Ethan or Walter, so I did not want to make her feel left out.

"Hello," I said, extending my hand and giving her a friendly smile. "I'm Angel."

"Hi, I'm Monica, Ethan's friend," she said as she politely shook my hand. She didn't seem to know me, however I did see what I could have sworn was a flicker of something when I said my name. I was sure that motor-mouth Ethan had told her about my meeting up with them at the restaurant.

"So, how is he?" I asked.

"We don't know yet," Stacey said, taking a seat on one of the waiting room chairs.

We both followed her lead and sat down, each of us taking a seat on either side of her.

"The good thing is that we were lucky he lives where he does," she continued. "I mean, his apartment complex is right next door to the hospital. As soon as his neighbors heard the shots, they called the police. The ambulance got to him pretty quickly and they rushed him right over here."

"That's great," I said, rubbing her arm. "Hopefully he was able to get the treatment he needed in time." I instantly regretted my words the minute they left my lips

"Yeah, hopefully," she said, her body slumping. "Hopefully."

Our group was silent for a few minutes as the awkwardness of my words seemed to bounce through the air around us.

Sensing something was wrong, Ethan and Greg walked back over to us and sat down in the rows of chairs facing ours.

"You know you don't have any home training, right?" Greg said in his usual loud voice, looking directly at Ethan.

"Man, what are you talking about?" Ethan asked, turning to look at each of us to see if we knew why Greg made the comment.

"Excuse me, ma'am," Greg said, ignoring Ethan as he got up and took the empty seat next to Monica.

"Yes, how may I help you, Greg?" she asked, batting her eyes exaggeratedly and flashing a big smile at him.

"Oh, you know my name," Greg said as he extended his hand to her. "It's kind of sad that I don't know yours though. It seems our mutual friend with his rude behind hasn't taken the time to introduce us."

"Yes, he's rude like that, isn't he?" she said, shaking his hand, "I'm Monica. It's so very nice to finally meet a real gentleman. There are far too few of you guys left in the world."

Ethan was looking back and forth between both of them like they were crazy.

"You know what," he said as he stood to his feet with a big smile on his face, "both of y'all can kiss all of my Jamaican born as—"

"Walter? Walter Johnson?" a heavy set nurse called out. She entered the waiting room, wearing a pair of bright blue medical scrubs and holding a clipboard.

"Hey, that's Viola," Ethan whispered to Greg, snapping his fingers as he recognized the nurse. "That's the chick I was telling you about earlier. Pinky, remember?"

"Word?" Greg said. "That's right. You did say that she worked here."

"Right here," Stacey said, standing up and giving Ethan and Greg a stern look before walking over to the nurse.

We all silently followed behind her, hoping to get some good news about our friend.

36

Walter

*T*he loud blasts from the powerful air horn echoed throughout the port. The sound brought cheers from the crowd gathered on the deck of the massive cruise ship. With that loud and clear signal, our cruise was finally about to be underway.

Standing with my friends as we all gathered together on the cruise ship's Lido deck, I was leaning on the rail and watching the workers scurrying around on the dock below. They had just finished removing the huge blue ropes that tethered the boat to the dock and we were ready to set sail. A few moments later, the entire ship shuddered briefly as its huge engines throttled up. Slowly, we began to move away from the dock and a few minutes later, the big ship was travelling down the wide channel, picking up speed as it headed out to deep water.

We were sailing parallel to the road which was the main artery that connected the port to the mainland. The Miami skyline in the distance was a hazy blur in the bright afternoon sunshine, enhancing what was already an absolutely beautiful day. Enjoying the moment, I was glad I had made the decision to go on the cruise even though I was still in pain and recovering from my injuries.

Ethan came up with the idea that instead of all of us staying at home and doing a traditional Thanksgiving holiday, we would go on a cruise to the Bahamas. With all of the excitement that had happened in the past few weeks, he felt that a cruise would be a great time for us to be together as friends, give thanks, and also have some fun and relaxation.

Being that my left arm was in a sling, it was difficult to find a way to lean comfortably against the railing. Finally finding a suitable position, I gazed out at the beautiful Miami coastline and thought about all of the many things that I did indeed have to give thanks for. I looked down at the water below churning against the hull of the ship and thought back to the fateful night that I returned home to find Darlene there waiting on me.

I recalled the paralyzing fear that gripped my body as I looked down the gaping barrel of the gun that she pointed at me. I could never forget the look on her face which was a mixture of anger, love, and hatred.

I subconsciously winced as I remembered the searing, burning pain that racked my body as each bullet pierced my skin. I remembered collapsing and watching through blurring vision my blood as it pooled on the carpet around me.

I lost almost two pints of blood and probably would have lost more if the paramedics hadn't shown up as quickly as they did. They stabilized me and rushed me to the hospital. Once there, the took me straight to the emergency room where I underwent three hours of surgery, during which, the doctors pulled two bullets out of my body.

Darlene had shot me three times, but luckily only two of the bullets actually ended up in me. The bullet that went into my left arm did some minor muscle damage, but that was nothing in comparison to the bullet that struck me in the left shoulder. It shattered my collarbone and did major nerve damage, making it difficult for me to move my arm. The doctor told me that if that bullet had hit me about six inches lower than it did, it would have punctured my heart and probably killed me instantly. The third bullet only grazed my right thigh and caused more discomfort than anything else.

I took a deep breath of the fresh air whipping by my face and I thought about all of the things that could have happened but didn't.

I was alive, Darlene was not. The sadness that hit me at the thought of her being dead was quickly replaced by anger. Not so much anger at her and the things that she did during our time together or the events of that disastrous day, but the feeling of anger was directed at myself.

As I lay in the hospital recuperating those many days after the shooting, I had plenty of time to think about how I allowed things to develop, to fester, to reach the point they did.

I was a punk when it came to Darlene. Instead of being a man and being more assertive in my interactions with her, I instead took the passive approach and did not speak to my real feelings. Things spiraled out of control and the end result was me in the hospital and Darlene in the morgue.

I closed my eyes and shuddered at the memory of Darlene's casket being slowly lowered into the ground that chilly Friday afternoon two weeks ago. Only fifteen or so people came to the funeral ceremony and they were mainly her coworkers. Only a few of her family or friends were there, which made the already sad occasion even more so.

For several days after the funeral, I asked myself the honest question: *Did I love her?* It bothered me that after all the time we had been together, the good times, the bad times, I still could not quickly and easily answer the question. I knew there was something there between us, but was it really love?

I shook these sad thoughts out of my head, opened my eyes, looked to my left, and smiled as I gazed at my future. I studied Stacey as she leaned with her back to the railing, looking at the calypso band singing and playing reggae music on the stage set up under the huge television monitor on the ship's deck.

As I took in her beauty, her happy smile, her alluring features, there was no doubt that I loved her. I didn't have to ponder this at all. I loved her and was in love with her.

The entire episode with me getting shot had brought us closer together than either of us could have imagined. We had not known each other for that long, but we quickly developed something that took other people years to cultivate. I have tried several times to put what we had into words, but at the end of the day, our business meeting over lunch at Applebee's was the spark of a romance which burst into the roaring flames of love the night that Darlene pulled the trigger.

I looked at Ethan standing to my right, his arm draped over Monica as he pointed at something in the distance. The two of them had fallen in love so deeply. It was unmistakable that they were perfect for each other. I love my boy like a brother and I was happy that he had this special woman come into his life.

Monica was laughing at something Ethan was saying to her and that in turn brought a smile to my face. I took a liking to Monica the minute I met her. He brought her with him on one of his many visits to see me when I was in the hospital. She could flow with Ethan's silly sense of humor and was the type of intelligent woman that could keep his attention and stimulate him in the way that he needed.

I looked beyond them to Evan who was saying something to Greg. Greg's attention however was focused on the couple standing beside Stacey. He had a vicious scowl on his face which revealed the emotional pain I knew he still felt each time he saw Angel and Cory together. He was recovering from the crushing way she ended things with him. Where he thought they were beginning to get closer to each other and really develop their secret relationship into something meaningful, Angel on the other hand had other ideas.

On one of his visits, Ethan relayed the sad story about Greg and Angel. A week after the night that they ran into each other in Quip, she invited him over to her house saying they needed to talk. Every guy knows that when a woman says that she needs to talk, the news which follows is probably not going to be something he wants to hear. This was definitely true in Greg's case because instead of Angel telling him that she was sick, pregnant, or anything else in between, she dropped something even more devastating on him.

She unceremoniously told him that she didn't want them to be involved anymore in any type of a relationship. After looking at me laying in the hospital with tubes running into my body, she realized just how short life was. She said that as she rode home in his terrible excuse for a car, she made her decision right then and there that she wanted to make sure she had the fullest life possible. She said that it wasn't an easy decision because she really did have feelings for Greg, but she had to do what she felt was best for her

I looked over at Angel, who was standing on the railing beside Stacey as they both watched the band play. I was disappointed at the fact that deep down, she didn't care for the guy who she dumped Greg to be with.

Cory, standing beside Angel, had his arm wrapped tightly around her waist as if telling the world that she was with him. I wasn't surprised at all when Ethan called to tell me that not only was Angel still going on the cruise after she and Greg ended their thing, but she was going to bring Cory along with her. He said they had gotten a junior suite and would be flying first class to Miami, all of which of course, would be paid for by Cory.

Cory was the epitome of a metrosexual and looked like he had called a fashion consultant and asked them to dress him in cruise attire. He had on excruciatingly tight white pants rolled up at the ankles, a blue Hawaiian luau shirt, boat shoes without socks, a Kangol cap, and aviator shades. The way that Greg was looking at him, I think that if we weren't standing between him and Cory, he probably would have pushed him over the railing. I hoped that Cory could swim because we had four more days on the ship and I didn't completely rule out that it might indeed happen.

Greg wasn't doing too badly though. Angel actually miscalculated when she chose to leave him and get with Cory. Two days after she ended things with him, Greg stopped at a convenience store on his way home from work. On a whim, he decided to put five dollars on the lottery. A few days later when the quick pick numbers on one of his Fantasy Five lottery tickets matched the winning numbers, he was the instant winner of $197,000.

I looked at my friends standing on either side of me, talking amongst each other. It felt good to be with this exceptional group of people. I knew the next few days were going to make for special memories which we would never soon forget.

Right as the ship left the mouth of the bay and entered into the Atlantic Ocean, Ethan stepped away from the railing, called out to us, and held up his Mai Tai.

"That's a pretty fruity drink you have there, Sir," Greg said, causing us to break into laughter. "I mean damn. You've got your pinky all tooted up and everything."

"Why are we friends?" Ethan said in mock exasperation.

As our laughter died down, he took a long look at each of us, as if trying to preserve the moment before he spoke.

"I wanted to thank all of you for coming out," he said. "These last few months have brought us joy, love, pleasure, and pain. I'm so glad that we're here on this Thanksgiving weekend, to give thanks for everything we have. We're truly blessed to be alive, to be healthy, to be able to love, to be loved. We've been through some tough times and I know our love and friendship will see us through whatever rough times lay ahead."

"Cheers!" he said, raising his glass.

"Cheers!" we all said in unison, raising our glasses and joining him in the toast.

The End

Made in the USA
Columbia, SC
31 December 2019